To Julia,
you are th[e]
XX Edge!. Tha[nk]
you for all your work.
XO, Ruth

You will see yourself,
in the books pages!
You are the XX Edge
Indeed

Patience

Praise for *The XX Edge*

"*The XX Edge* is a 'get behind' kind of book. Marime-Ball and Shaber draw on their extensive research and real world experience to make a compelling argument for more gender inclusivity when it comes to business and the economy. It is a must-read for every leader who wants to deliver stronger long-term performance and positive and inclusive societal outcomes. It should be in the hands of every citizen who aspires to effect positive change."

   –JAMES MANYIKA, Chair and Director Emeritus,
     McKinsey Global Institute

"The authors paint a powerfully persuasive picture of the results when women are at the centre of investing, as agents and actors. At last, we can understand the vast difference that women can make to the effectiveness of the financial world in meeting the challenges ahead. This book is vital reading for anyone concerned about the future of finance."

   –DR. SCILLA ELWORTHY, Three-time Nobel Peace Prize
     Nominee, Founder of The Oxford Research Group and
     Peace Direct, and Author of *The Business Plan for Peace*

"As the world is witnessing unprecedented technological change, the question of how innovation can serve more people is front and center. This book makes a strong case for how products and services are more inclusive and higher quality when women are inside innovation labs."

   –WILLIAM SONNEBORN, Senior Director, Disruptive
     Technologies and Funds, International Finance
     Corporation

THE
XX
EDGE

UNLOCKING
HIGHER RETURNS AND
LOWER RISK

Patience Marime-Ball *and* Ruth Shaber, MD

Worth
BOOKS

Published by Worth Books.

ISBN: 978-1-63763-093-8 (Print)
ISBN: 978-1-63763-094-5 (eBook)

Cover Design by Bruce Gore, Gore Studio Inc.

*Dedicated to all the changemakers
and to our mothers:
Farirai Pfupajena, teacher, and Betty Miller Ball,
champion of changemakers
Sandra Shaber—economist, feminist, and proud capitalist*

TABLE OF CONTENTS

INTRODUCTION

I F YOU ARE MANAGING INVESTMENTS, EITHER YOUR own or on behalf of clients, your primary goal is to generate the best returns possible and grow these assets. What most investors don't realize is that when more women are involved in financial decision-making across all entities that make financial decisions (including governments, private and public companies, investment funds, real estate development, and individual households), money is managed more efficiently and effectively, investments are more profitable, and companies and governments make better decisions that benefit individual investors and, ultimately, the overall economy. You can put this knowledge to use. This is what we call the "XX Edge."

MORE PIE FOR EVERYONE

Investing is not a zero-sum game. Untapped investment opportunities can be found at the intersection of gender and finance. Nevertheless, many investors still base their investing decisions on the notion that the total amount of the world's assets is fixed and that if one investor is gaining, another must be losing. Milton Friedman memorably wrote in 1980, "Most economic fallacies derive from the tendency to assume that there is a fixed pie, that one party can gain only at the expense of another."[1] Instead, expanding the use of diverse talent in financial decision-making optimizes returns, grows the overall economy, and extends more opportunity to everyone. Optimizing human talent leads to more innovation and results in expanding financial returns for investors. Women's leadership skills are currently underutilized across all capital markets. Women represent only a small fraction of the individuals making the financial decisions that impact domestic and global economies. This underutilization leads to inefficiencies and missed opportunities in the markets. In general, women are poised to tackle the challenges ahead of us because they are closer to most of the problems that need to be solved, utilize collaborative leadership styles, are more aware of risks (and therefore conduct due diligence and prioritize investment allocation differently), and take the long view in financial decisions. Women's financial leadership will lead to more innovation, stronger investment returns, and accelerated economic growth.

When the financial services industry successfully includes women in decision-making roles and optimizes their skills across all capital markets, the individual investor will enjoy higher returns and benefit from the innovation and economic growth. Diversity makes the team stronger and offers you and others better returns. Those who are open to innovative ideas from all sources and who have confidence in their own potential while understanding that a more diverse team does not take them out of the game are positioned to capitalize on this opportunity and dramatically grow their wealth.

A NEW PARADIGM FOR
GENDER-FOCUSED INVESTING

The field of gender-focused investing is about to be flipped. Traditionally, the field has prioritized how finance can improve the lives of women and girls and thereby lift families and communities. Consider a different paradigm: one with women at the center of investing as agents and actors, not just as beneficiaries.

Gender analysis is the secret to unlocking better financial performance for all investors. The evidence is clear that when women share in the control of capital (as board directors, CEOs, entrepreneurs, borrowers, heads of government), better social and financial outcomes are the result.[2] Furthermore, when women are included in decision-making, they build solutions that also benefit their families and communities. When women have access to more money, they build wealthier and healthier economies—at family, community, national, and global levels. They make the economy grow and bring better outcomes to everyone. To be clear, this new paradigm demands we move away from the idea that microfinance is the only type of capital that we associate with women. We must open all types of capital to the full participation of women and have them involved in all allocation decisions.

Today only a small percentage of women participate in significant financial industry decision-making. Of the Fortune 500 companies, only 41 are led by women.[3] Barely 14% of private equity fund managers are women, and less than 3% of venture capital is directed toward enterprises run by women.[4]

Why would women's financial decision-making lead to better financial and social performance? Data indicates that more diversity in leadership brings additional talented people into company decision rooms, investment committee meetings, and public policy forums.[5] Women tend to prioritize long-term outcomes and take on risk in a different way than men. Women bring distinct types of innovation and creativity to problem-solving because they directly experience the impact of the challenges that need to be addressed. And women tend to exhibit collaborative network leadership styles that are well suited to our changing global economy.[6]

To accrue higher returns and lower risks, the world of finance must fully appreciate that including talented women in decision-making positions is the secret to unlocking better financial returns. When all members of the investment community prioritize investments that place female talent at the table, demand for women board directors and CEOs will grow. This will drive pay equity at the top and throughout organizations and will generate a pipeline of talent in middle management, vocational schools, and universities. There will be a demand for female fund managers and entrepreneurs who will bring untapped venture capital to the hands of more female innovators and disruptors. This, in turn, will result in product development, services, and strategies that cost-effectively meet the needs of all, such as new forms of effective and safe contraception, more climate-friendly consumer goods, and financial products that reach those who are traditionally excluded. Women will be prioritized as business owners and mortgage holders, which will result in more reliable loan repayments and more stable neighborhoods and towns. This is just the beginning of how our economy will improve when women make more financial decisions and exert more control over the flow of capital. As an investor, you will want to take full advantage of this expansive and developing opportunity.

WHAT YOU WILL FIND IN THIS BOOK
In the chapters to come, we will outline data, research, and case stories to build your understanding of gender-focused investing. We will examine the inherent gender differences between women and men and consider why these differences make women effective and efficient financial decision-makers. We will look at the evidence that proves this point across all asset classes. We'll look at the environmental, social, and governance contexts that shape current and future investment opportunities, including the financial risks of not fully implementing this new paradigm. We'll take you through some examples of how giving women financial decision-making power generates solutions to some of the world's most pressing problems. Finally, we will give you some specific and actionable opportunities to implement what you learn from this book.

But before we get into these details, let us introduce ourselves and our backgrounds so you can understand why we wrote this book.

RUTH'S JOURNEY

Throughout my professional career, both as an obstetrician/gynecologist and a health-care executive, one thing has been clear to me: the best way to improve people's lives and solve complex problems is to engage women. Use their talents and let them be the levers of change. When a woman is healthy, her family is more likely to be healthy. When women have access to noncoercive family planning that allows them to control when and how to have children, they are more likely to optimize not only their own economic and social outcomes but those of their families and communities at the same time. Women ensure that their family members have adequate health care. When women have information and resources, they are more likely to be financially accountable—whether in service to their families, their own enterprises, their communities, or their governments.

I retired from my career in medicine in 2012. When I launched my new career as a philanthropist and impact investor, I saw endless opportunities to elevate women as agents of change to solve the world's problems. I founded the Tara Health Foundation, where we developed an integrated capital model that matches the appropriate type of capital (such as charitable grants, recoverable grants, loans, or equity investments) to each problem, putting women at the center of the process. When we turned our attention to the public markets, we focused on developing the tools and processes for evaluating companies that are good places for women to work and have a positive impact on their communities. These tools are now publicly available to any investor. By using a gender analysis across our entire portfolio, we have had returns on our investments that consistently beat market benchmarks—an exciting result. I am confident that the Tara Health Foundation investment portfolio overperforms because of our gender focus.

PATIENCE'S JOURNEY

I was born in Zimbabwe, educated in Europe and the United States, and started my investing career in 1996 at the International Finance Corporation (IFC), the private sector arm of the World Bank Group. It was a fantastic job that allowed me to make investments at the intersection of economic capacity, strong financial returns, and legal rights. My work spanned investments in infrastructure, nonperforming investments, and financial institutions. In 2008 I was working in IFC's financial markets group when the subprime crisis unfolded. It was the beginning of my deeper understanding of the value of women's leadership. About that time, Christine Lagarde, the head of the International Monetary Fund, said, "If it had been Lehman Sisters rather than Lehman Brothers, the world might well look a lot different today."[7] I started looking at the performance differences and learned that companies with gender-diverse leadership were faring better with more stable earnings and stock prices relative to their peers. They also emerged from the crisis faster than peers without gender-diverse leadership. I saw how "Lehman Brothers and Sisters" would have been a better investment bank. After reviewing the viability of building a business for IFC focused on prioritizing the role of women economic actors, I developed and built IFC's Banking on Women business unit, choosing a name that played on the opportunity of counting on women and providing women with access to bank capital. Today it is a multibillion-dollar business for IFC. We issued the first-ever gender bond and developed the first global debt fund, sized at $600 million, focused on investing in women entrepreneurs. As of June 2021, the Banking on Women platform has facilitated the investment of over $15.6 billion in women entrepreneurs around the world.

In my career at IFC I worked and traveled extensively around the world. I had two sons who had grown up with a mom who was often away from home. In 2014, I took early retirement to spend more time with my two Black sons before they headed off to college, being present in their lives and cooking dinner. I also started investing in gender-diverse founder teams as an angel investor. I joined a team that was raising their second venture fund, and we struggled to raise the capital. It was frustrating to see how institutional investors viewed the female opportunity as mostly a microcredit opportunity rather than a profit-making opportunity. This helped me see the critical need for a 100% gender-focused institutional pool of capital with the intention of investing in women who are driving solutions. It needed to operate across the capital spectrum, from early stage investing to public equities. I took some money from my pension fund and used it to start the Women of the World Endowment (WoWE), a 501(c)(3) focused on raising a significant, evergreen endowment to invest in women changemakers who are building solutions for the world's most pressing environmental, social, and governance challenges. We invest the endowment capital for risk-adjusted returns, as with any market strategy. We also look for deep impact returns. We collaborate with and influence other investors to fund strategies that fully centralize women as decision-makers, and we use the income generated from our investments to provide grants to women-focused systems orchestrators, organizations that are removing barriers and driving large-scale change.

WoWE is a bold idea. Our ambition is to build a $5 billion, 100% mission-aligned endowment. Many doubt that we will achieve this ambition because I am a woman, a Black woman, an African woman who is focused on the idea of mainstreaming investing in and through women. It will be hard to achieve this ambition, but I do not doubt that we will be successful. The time has come for this significant ambition. Women changemakers, with the right allies, are getting bold things done.

OUR PARTNERSHIP

Why the two of us? How did two people from quite different backgrounds end up working toward the same ambitious goal? Our professional journeys were different, but we were both rare breeds. We worked in areas that denied women equal seats at the table or space in innovation labs, despite our talent.

We came together in 2019. We are collaborators in a relationship based on mutual respect. We recognize each other's power and realize that the gender movement has for a long time been exclusive, reserved for white women as leaders of the movement and beneficiaries of any seats created at the tables of power.[8] We want to change that.

In our separate careers and differing fields of expertise, we have demonstrated that collaborative leadership can create more health and wealth. We have had a common approach in harnessing the power to change systems and putting women at the center of decision-making. We are working together on this book to explore applications from our knowledge of the finance industry, the global economy, and the human condition. Our experience and success in investing at the intersection of gender, economic, and social impact will benefit all future investors.

A WORD ABOUT GENDER

In the history of gender-focused investing, most conversations about it have been among women. Therefore, this book will provide women with additional information to confirm what they have known all along. Mothers, sisters, and daughters are aware that they are running operations in their homes, building innovative solutions in communities, and holding up skies across continents.

However, because men make most of the investment decisions in the world, we see them as the most essential audience for this book. If you are a man reading this book, we thank you for taking the time to broaden your viewpoint and the returns on your investment portfolio. Men have been managing the world's economies and been in control of global financial decision-making for thousands of years. Despite some difficulties along the way, the world has gotten much better over the course of human history. As Steven Pinker outlines so well in *Enlightenment Now,*

"For all the flaws in human nature, it contains the seeds of its own improvement."[9] Over the past thousand years, we've seen dramatic improvement across every measure of the human condition, including life expectancy, poverty alleviation, human rights, violence, and literacy. For all our focus on the challenges ahead, we want to express gratitude for the innovative men who have seized opportunities and created a better world. We hope that the same spirit of innovation and hard work will extend to engaging all human talent if we are to fully address the environmental and social challenges in this next chapter of human history.

And now a note about gender. In these pages, we categorize some people as "women." This book makes the case that financial decision-making should be shifted to people who identify as female, regardless of their biological sex. This includes both cis and trans women. However, the evidence that we cite is limited because it is based on studies of cis women. Furthermore, our descriptions and characterizations are as tendencies, not absolutes. All people are individuals and should be treated as such. Traits that we've described as female are not limited to cis women. Trans people, nonbinary people, and men can have these traits too. We've made the intentional decision to use the word *women*, but we know that it's not inclusive. While we focus on women's financial leadership in this book, many of the findings are transferable to everyone who is underrepresented at capital-allocation tables. When diverse talent can share in financial decision-making and leadership, we all benefit.

In the following chapters, you will see the evidence that when the financial industry recruits more talented women to leadership positions, all investors will realize better financial returns. Whether you are managing your own money or someone else's, whether you are running a billion-dollar public company or the budget for a small household, whether you are making purchasing decisions for a state government or buying for yourself from a local farmers market, having women at every point of the value chain will enhance your personal returns and grow the economy for all to benefit. This book is about the consistent financial edge of this more inclusive approach.

The potential impact is huge. When women sit at the table, we all benefit—the social, environmental, and economic benefits are clear. We can make the pie bigger for all of us.

Now, let's get to work.

CHAPTER 1

THE LEADERSHIP EDGE

MORE MONEY, MORE IMPACT

WHY ARE OUTCOMES BETTER WHEN MORE WOMEN control more capital? What is it about women that makes them great financial decision-makers? In this section we discuss three key opportunities that investors are missing and three inherent gender differences that investors are not tapping into that answer these questions.

First, female talent is vastly underutilized. Only 5% of chief executive officers (CEOs), fund managers, or venture capital recipients are women, which means a significant amount of talent is excluded from these roles and left out of innovation, decision-making, and capital allocation.[10] When this human capital is applied to problem-solving, better outcomes are the result.

Second, when products are designed without including female innovators and female end users, opportunities are missed and products are not broadly successful. Only a foolish investor fails to include a gender analysis when investing in new products or services.

Third, women are terrific problem-solvers because they are closer to so many of the crises that need to be addressed. In the areas of education, health care, urban planning, and nutrition, women are not only frontline workers but make up the majority of users and consumers. This makes them well positioned to solve the fundamental problems that plague these sectors. Performance improvement research from the health-care sector has demonstrated that when frontline teams help solve systemic problems, the outcomes are more positive and sustainable.[11] Because of their proximity to these challenges, women are essential contributors to all product designs. In the financial markets, we find that women's solutions to entrenched problems tend to emphasize long-term sustainability and risk mitigation, generating strong overall financial returns.[12]

Research has shown us that when women are included in capital management, they bring the benefit of inherent gender differences that lead to long-term positive outcomes. In part, this is because women tend to have smaller ego needs than men, so they have collaborative, networking leadership styles that are well suited to bringing people together to fix the world's most pressing problems.

Next, women are more risk aware. They do their research when reviewing or investing in an opportunity. This means they understand the financial, environmental, and social risks that are inherent in business or government decisions.

And finally, women are more likely to take the long view. They avoid decisions that prioritize short-term gains at the expense of long-term success. In financial markets, we see that when women can innovate and provide solutions to entrenched problems, they invest in long-term sustainable solutions and avoid risk, which results in strong overall financial returns.[13]

THE OPPORTUNITIES:
TAPPING INTO MORE TALENT
Diversity of Talent: An Inclusive Model with More Upside
This book specifically advocates for gender diversity in financial decision-making. Diversity matters as there is overwhelming evidence that teams composed of individuals from many different backgrounds in addition to gender (such as race, geography, disability, and age) outperform across multiple dimensions. As we review the evidence

to support this, we will sometimes refer to research on gender diversity and sometimes to data on racial diversity. While our sources are not limited to gender analysis, most patterns seen with racial diversity measures are transferable to gender.

Some might argue that if civilization has come this far with an exclusive and discriminatory operating model (that is, with white men making most of the world's financial decisions), does diversity of talent even matter? We think that we would have progressed much further as a civilization if everyone were empowered to make such decisions. As a Black woman who has the lived experience of both gender and racial exclusion and discrimination, I (Patience) would posit that it matters not because I would prefer that opportunity was equally available to me but because increased diversity across all industries, job roles, decision-making rooms, and every country in the world would yield significantly stronger financial and social dividends, including health and wealth at the individual level. The data illustrates this, and we will explore such data more in this book. What is intriguing is how, with all the data we have and the visual of 2020 where we saw previously "invisible" talent taking on critical and essential roles, the world has not broadly embraced a full-potential-of-all-talent operating model.

In a recent television interview, Bryan Caplan, an economics professor at George Mason University, posed a provocative question that may shed light on how the opportunity of greater talent inclusion is perceived: "How can we tell that something that helps some people and hurts others is overall a good thing?" His question was related to his book *Open Borders: The Science and Ethics of Immigration*, but it fits well in any situation in which there is a perceived zero-sum outcome.[14] In the case of an inclusive talent model, applying his question would mean that those who would benefit are currently excluded and those who would be hurt are currently included. But Mr. Caplan's question assumes lower financial returns, a static or shrinking opportunity set, and a fixed economic pie. This assumption explains what is holding the world back from an inclusive talent operating model and the potential for better returns and accelerated growth it could bring. Fundamental to the inclusive talent operating model is that it brings better social outcomes for more communities and makes a bigger economic pie overall. The question: what will it take for the world to recognize this? When will it act accordingly? The answer: when each of you as reader and investor makes investing decisions that fully capture the upside potential of women as decision-makers, leaders, asset allocators, innovators, and full members of all levels of society.

Investing into a structurally unequal system creates friction that works against better financial performance and economic growth. For example, if we consider home ownership as a marker of control of capital at the individual level, the average person who owned a home at the beginning of the 2020 pandemic is relatively wealthier today. On the other hand, people who rent have been excluded from this form of wealth attainment, some of whom may have lost their jobs and moved to live with family, sometimes placing themselves further away from employment opportunities. In more extreme cases they may have become homeless and are now unable to provide an address to a potential employer. These people may have, for the medium to long term, lost the opportunity to join the workforce and will have further to climb to get back to their pre-pandemic economic status.[15] The longer they are out of full employment, the harder it becomes to reenter the workforce. As economic activity has picked up again, employers are looking for talent and having a tough time finding it, resulting in negative pressure on profits. These phenomena create drag at a macroeconomic level as well as an individual business level. If we had entered the pandemic period with less structural inequity, we would have less drag as we begin to build back and accelerate GDP growth. Fortunately, this is addressable drag. If we collectively commit to a full potential operating model and take steps to implement necessary changes, we can position large parts of economies for growth. Doing so may be tough in the short term, but the results will be better in the long term.

What would these changes look like? In a June 2021 *Barron's* conversation titled "Moving from Talk to Action," Calvin Butler, CEO of Exelon Utilities, an energy generation company, talked about the work Exelon has been doing to build an inclusive workforce.[16] It was clear that the company executives were intentional about the inclusive program and specified strategies for hiring, including a requirement that all company job offerings have diverse candidates in the short list and all interview panels be diverse.

"From those requirements, we get a diverse workforce," said Butler. "When you have diverse slates and interview panels, diverse talent gets hired." This philosophy is paying off for Exelon. Butler indicated that since starting this work, Exelon has experienced the highest service reliability and highest customer satisfaction ratings in company history while receiving recognition as a top place to work. The company has gone further and created a diversity honor roll. It now ranks its bankers, lawyers, and money managers on the diversity of the teams working on Exelon's business.[17]

Another example comes from the world's largest pension fund, the $1.7 trillion Government Pension Investment Fund (GPIF) of Japan. GPIF requires its fund managers to explain how they are incorporating gender considerations in their investment processes.[18] When GPIF first rolled out this requirement, managers pushed back, arguing that this would take time to implement. The response from GPIF leadership was that the failure of fund managers to take gender into consideration created a material risk that would undermine their credibility and jeopardize their long-term contracts with GPIF. Given this position, the fund managers figured out how to develop the necessary strategies to meet the requirement.[19] In 2021, I (Patience) spoke on a panel at the largest impact investing conference in Japan. I saw how these requests by asset owners are having some impact in the market. While too many gender-focused conversations have traditionally involved women panelists speaking to a female audience, this panel had two female and two male speakers. The conversation covered the need for increased diversity at all levels in companies as well as data disclosure that can lead to differentiated investment strategies and products. As these types of interventions become more routine, the friction against accruing greater returns and growing the economic pie through a more inclusive talent model will be removed (see the case story of GPIF in chapter 5).

The preceding examples are but a few of many that show us that it is possible for companies and investors to move toward inclusive models. These efforts should be commonplace. What entity does not want better financial and workforce productivity returns, such as Exelon, or what asset owner does not want to have better risk-mitigation structures, such as GPIF. This matters to the long-term health of the individual investment portfolio and the growth of economies.

Let's take a look at gross world product, sometimes called global GDP. This is the sum of all the goods and services produced in the world and can be thought of as the pie we all share. Projections by major economic research bodies have long indicated that an inclusive talent model would cause global GDP to grow. A 2015 McKinsey Global Institute report that studied 95 countries found that, if we had reached full gender equality starting in 2015, global GDP would have increased by up to US$28 trillion by 2025.[20] McKinsey also provided more conservative estimates that are still impressive. If every country in this sample of 95 had kept pace with its fastest-improving neighbor on the list regarding gender parity in the workforce, global GDP would have increased by up to US$12 trillion in a ten-year period.[21] A 2017 report from S&P Global stated that a sustained effort to increase women's entry into and retention in the workforce could add 5 to 10% in nominal GDP to the world's principal economies in just a few decades.[22]

The review for country-level estimates reveals the same. The 2017 S&P Global report estimated that the US economy could have been $1.6 trillion larger in 2017 if women had entered and remained in the workforce at the same rates as women did in a country such as Norway, which consistently outpaces the United States when it comes to women in the workforce.[23] More recent estimates from a 2021 study by the Federal Reserve Bank of San Francisco estimate that closing race and gender gaps in employment at all levels would have generated $2.6 trillion in additional economic output in the United States in 2019 *alone*.[24] Cumulative gains from 1990 through 2019 would have amounted to about $70 trillion in additional output.[25]

Like the 2008 financial crisis period, the pandemic that began in 2020 has led to significant economic stimuli by governments around the world. We wonder if the world would have needed so much stimulus if global economies had been operating with a full talent paradigm. With more people gainfully employed and more talent engaged in developing solutions to address health- and climate-related challenges, people would be healthier, wealthier, and better positioned to overcome the effects of the pandemic and other natural disasters at an individual level, mitigating the need for significant government-level interventions.

An eye-opening 2018 study by the International Monetary Fund (IMF) found that the economic growth from having women enter the workforce isn't all derived from the benefits of a larger workforce, as women and men are not "standard" units of labor that bring the exact same skills and strengths to their work.[26] For countries that scored worse on gender inequality in the workforce, for example, closing that gender gap could increase national GDPs by 35% on average.[27] The IMF estimated that at least 20% of the GDP increase would be due to the ways gender diversity, particularly the different skill sets and strengths that women bring to the workforce, amp up productivity.[28] While some might worry that an expanded workforce results in a decline in average wages, the increase in productivity drives wages up for both men and women. Translating current welfare gaps from women's exclusion from the workforce into potential gains, some countries could see a welfare gain of as much as 20% if they removed barriers to an inclusive workforce.[29] That's a health and wealth gain for *everyone*, not just women. In a later section of this chapter, we will elaborate on how gender differences can be used to grow the economic pie faster and in a more resilient way.

We need inclusive talent models across the spectrum, including in leadership positions and in boardrooms. In a survey published in 2021, commissioned by Bank of America, companies where a board's gender diversity is above the median enjoyed a 15% higher return on equity (ROE) and a "50% lower earnings risk one year out compared with their less diverse peers."[30] Not only are boards with more women seeing better overall performance, but boards with fewer women are losing out. Having diverse talent grows the pie for all, yet only 11 of the companies in the S&P 500 Index have equally balanced male/female boards.[31] Only 8 have leadership teams where at least half the members are women.[32]

For a company to enjoy optimum success, it must emphasize diverse talent in its management positions as well as its lower ranks. Diverse teams tend to outperform nondiverse teams across various metrics, including downside risk mitigation, better innovation, and financial performance. Credit Suisse's 2019 Gender 3000 report found that from 2010 to 2019, companies around the world with higher proportions of women in management (i.e., greater than 17% of their management teams) had consistently better performance than those with lower proportions.[33] According to the report, companies with women comprising 20% or more of their management teams saw, on average, 3.6% better share price performance than companies with management teams of less than 15% women.[34] The 2021 Bank of America report mentioned found that companies with above-median levels of women in management saw 30% higher returns on equity and 30% lower earnings risk over one year than companies with below-median numbers of women in management positions.[35] And according to a 2009 study by University of Illinois–Chicago professor Cedric Herring, companies that scored highest on racial diversity generated almost 15 times more sales revenue than companies that scored lowest.[36]

On the innovation front, diverse teams are critical to staying ahead of competition because they lead to better new product development and more robust go-to-market strategies. A 2018 survey by the Boston Consulting Group and the Technical University of Munich of over 1,700 companies of varying industries and sizes across eight countries (the United States, France, Germany, China, Brazil, India, Switzerland, and Austria) found a statistically significant correlation between greater diversity in management and a higher proportion of the company's revenues generated by products and services developed in the last three years, which is a measure of innovation.[37] Companies with above-average diversity had on average a 19% higher proportion of revenues coming from innovation and 9%

higher earnings before interest and taxes (EBIT) margins, differences mostly attributable to diversity in industry, nationality, and gender.[38]

Even asset allocation receives a healthy boost in returns by including diverse talent. In venture capital, where the presence of diverse talent is woefully limited, data points to the same missed opportunities. Fostering diversity is a winning strategy. A 2018 *Harvard Business Review* study found a direct correlation between the diversity of venture capital investment partnerships and the success of the investments their teams chose. An investment's rate of comparative success increases by 26.4% if partnerships are made between people from different ethnic groups versus partnerships between people from the same ethnic group.[39] Increasing female partner hires by 10% resulted in an average 1.5% increase in overall fund returns and 9.7% more profitable exits for venture capital firms.[40] In a world where only about 28.8% of all venture capital investments result in profitable exits, those numbers are significant.[41] It's not that diverse teams were better at identifying worthwhile investments—venture projects selected by both homogenous and diverse investment teams appeared equal at first. Their performances diverged later, when investors began influencing portfolio company strategies, recruitment, and other critical dimensions of their development. In other words, the creativity and dynamism brought to the table by diverse investment teams made it significantly more likely for the companies they invested in to succeed in today's dynamic market context.[42]

The same dynamic shows up in local government, where community leaders make decisions that impact local communities. When women are involved in community leadership, more money is reinvested in their local communities and filtered into education, childcare, and other local infrastructure needs. In India, for example, women's representation in local government councils, known as *panchayats*, has led to an average implementation of 62% more drinking water projects than in areas without female representation. Droughts from climate change and sanitation needs from health-care crises such as the pandemic have demonstrated how even local-level infrastructure is critical to better overall welfare.[43]

In Norway, women's involvement in municipal councils resulted in better childcare facilities. We all now know how important childcare is having lived through 2020–2021 when the world became acutely aware of how childcare affected other economic sectors.[44]

These are just a few examples that show how applying an inclusive talent paradigm to financial decision-making provides significant tailwinds to individual investors and all economies and societies.

Product Design: New Opportunities and Risk Mitigation

When products and services are developed without women at the drafting table, without considering the impact of these products and services on women, literally half of the population's needs are not considered. People are harmed. Money is lost. Let's look at some examples.

Crash test dummies were first introduced in the 1950s to test automobile safety. These dummies were a remarkable innovation. They have saved countless lives by allowing car manufacturers to experiment with new safety mechanisms.

There's one problem: crash test dummies were designed to mimic the body size and shape of the average man.

The original research on how crashes affected the human body was conducted by Lawrence Patrick, a professor at Wayne State University. Initially, he subjected himself to crashes up to 45 mph. He also studied the effects of crashes on cadavers and animals. In the 1970s, one of Patrick's students, Harold Mertz, led a team at General Motors that designed the initial version of the male crash test dummy—the version that is still in use today. In 1973, the National Highway Traffic Safety Administration (NHTSA) began using data from simulated crashes using dummies to test and rate vehicle safety, creating a regulatory standard.[45]

For context, it's important to recognize that more attention was initially paid to male crash victims because men are more likely than women to be involved in a car crash—probably because they drive more frequently and more recklessly. Men are less likely to use seat belts, more likely to drive while impaired, and more likely to exceed speed limits.[46] Yet according to a 2011 study by University of Virginia researchers, when women are involved in crashes, they face a 47% higher chance of serious injury, 71% higher chance of moderate injury, and 17% higher chance of dying, even when controlling for height, weight, seat belt use, and crash intensity.[47] The imbalance in outcomes for women crash victims has more to do with women's anatomy and how cars are designed than how women drive.[48]

At first, most of the crash dummy design team, regulators, and executives at car manufacturers were men. There was one woman who weighed in on the decision to use male bodies as the prototype for the dummies. According to Joan Claybrook, administrator of the NHTSA in the late seventies and during the original testing and safety ratings by the government, the tests were conducted on male dummies because the agency had limited funds and because men were the ones who accounted for the highest absolute number of motor vehicle deaths (even though they were more likely to survive a crash).[49]

It's hard to know if the decision to base a whole generation of automobile safety products solely on the average male body might have been different if there had been women working in design, regulation, or automotive management. Male dummies are taller and heavier than most women and children, so the products that result from crash-test dummy testing didn't consider that women tend to sit closer to the steering wheel to reach the pedals, that women are more susceptible to whiplash because they have less muscle mass in their necks, or that woman ride in cars while pregnant.[50] The original crash test dummies didn't consider how pregnant women use seat belts and how their centers of gravity change as the pregnancy grows.[51]

One of the most important innovations that emerged during this period of safety testing was the driver and passenger airbag. Between 1970 and 1991, consumer safety groups, Congress, and lobbyists debated federal airbag requirements. In 1984, Federal Motor Vehicle Safety Standard 208 required all cars produced after April 1, 1989, have a passive restraint for the driver (airbag or seat belt). By 1991, passive restraints had to be in place for passengers.[52] While automakers were scrambling to integrate these safety features into their new cars, almost all of their product testing was conducted on either animals or dummies that were built to replicate a five-foot-nine, 165-pound man. Was harm done because of this oversight? According to the NHTSA, between 1987 and 2007, 75 out of the 98 driver fatalities due to air bag use in the United States were women. Of the 13 passenger fatalities, 11 were women.[53] Fortunately a push for second-generation airbags resulted in more protection for everyone.[54]

Airbags aren't the only car safety products designed to help only men. In the 1990s, automakers developed two kinds of safety systems to protect against whiplash. One absorbed crash energy in the seat back and head restraint. The other product used only a moving head restraint to diminish the movement of the head and neck in rear impact accidents. In both cases, these innovations primarily benefited male victims, with little or no protection for women.[55]

It took the contributions of female Swedish scientists Astrid Linder and Anna Carlsson to design and promote the use of crash test dummies that represented the sizes, shapes, and physiology of female drivers and passengers. Linder found that new cars with whiplash protection were being designed with men in mind. It's not surprising since crash test dummies were designed to mimic a male driver's relative weight and anatomy. "I saw information in the injury statistics showing that men were better protected from whiplash in the new systems and that women were still at higher risk. The goal is to make everyone in cars as well-protected as possible," Linder said.[56] "Hopefully a test method will evolve that also involves female dummies, which will prod car manufacturers into installing protection systems that automatically adjust the seats to each individual," Carlsson said. "Both men and women of various body sizes would benefit from that."[57]

In the early 1980s, researchers argued for the inclusion of 50th percentile female body sizes in the regulatory tests. The NHTSA (under Joan Claybrook's leadership) recognized the problem and tried to make up for this oversight by creating a "family" of dummies that included a small female, large male, and average female. Prototypes of the new dummies were built, but only the small female was used in the NHTSA's crash tests. The push to include dummies of multiple sizes and shapes was dropped in 1981 due to funding constraints and lack of prioritization of the impact of this technology on women. However, Linder and Carlsson are hopeful that more effective female dummies will be in use for official crash tests by 2030. It will take that long to formulate new regulations and test protocols.[58]

What was the collateral damage from designing safety products that accommodated only the male body? Well, thousands of women died unnecessarily. After identifying this problem, the automobile industry needed to scramble to invent second-generation products and other work-arounds (such as the passenger seat airbag "deactivation button") to mitigate the risks of an inadequately designed product. Would lives have been saved if women had been part of the original innovation team and had helped design a product that took gender into consideration? Definitely. The small investment in a more heterogeneous family of crash test dummies would have prevented the long-term loss of life and money.

There's another area where failure to involve women in product design has been even more lethal and costly: health care. Throughout the history of medical research and innovation, the female body and physiology have been treated as an afterthought. Historically, medical research took place on men and the findings were extrapolated to women. Even in animal testing, it is not unusual to have only male mice or other male laboratory animals as the surrogates for humans.[59] Why would this be so? It simplifies research to have homogenous subjects. Also, by excluding female animals and humans, there is no possibility of a pregnancy either skewing the research findings or, in the case of human research, inflicting damage on an undetected fetus.

One area where this approach has done the most harm is the study of heart disease. Cardiovascular disease (including heart attacks, heart failure, and strokes) has long been considered a disease of men, despite being the number one cause of death in American women.[60] Perhaps this perception is because men tend to have heart attacks at a younger age and are more likely to die earlier from heart disease.

Some of the original research (such as the Coronary Drug Project and the Physicians' Health Study) described the symptoms and manifestations of early heart disease in men only.[61] The exception to this focus on male hearts was the observation that women tended to develop heart disease ten years later than men, after they went through menopause. Based on observational studies in the 1960s and 1970s, it was concluded that natural estrogen exposure accounted for the delay in cardiovascular disease in women compared to men.[62] Without the benefit of a randomized clinical trial to test this hypothesis, doctors began to prescribe estrogen and progesterone (known as hormone therapy, or HT) not only to ameliorate the effects of decreased estrogen that occur at the time of menopause (such as hot flashes) but also to keep women's hearts and bones healthy and help them "stay young." The apparent benefits of the female hormone estrogen to prevent heart disease was so well assumed that the early clinical trials on estrogen and heart disease looked at whether men at risk for heart disease would benefit from taking it.

When I (Ruth) began my practice as an obstetrician and gynecologist in 1990, all women were encouraged to use postmenopausal HT—whether they were having menopausal symptoms or not. It was not until Bernadine Healy became the director of the US National Institutes of Health (NIH) in 1991 that research tested this assumption. Dr. Healy was a rare commodity in the 1970s and 1980s—a female cardiologist trained at Harvard Medical School and Johns Hopkins Hospital. After years in clinical practice that included serving as head of cardiac research at the Cleveland Clinic, she became the president of the American Heart Association in 1989. She was committed to convincing the public and the medical community that heart disease is not just a man's disease. As the first female director of the NIH in 1991, and with a budget of over $7 billion, she established a policy that the NIH would fund only those clinical trials that included both men and women when the condition being studied affects both sexes.[63] She changed established practice, and she had the funds to do it.

The recommendation to prescribe HT to almost all older women was dramatically reversed in 2002 when the shocking initial findings from the well-designed Women's Health Initiative were released. This randomized clinical trial found that the overall risk of heart attack for postmenopausal women increased when they took HT compared to a placebo.[64] In retrospect, the earlier observational studies erred by failing to distinguish causality from correlation and not fully accounting for selection bias in the study populations. What we have since learned from meticulously designed studies is that HT is harmful to many women, with the cardiac benefits limited to those women who have recently entered menopause.

We now know that the conventional teaching based on male physiology resulted in physicians ignoring or minimizing symptoms of heart disease in women. Women often have a different constellation of symptoms that go undiagnosed as heart disease when women come to emergency rooms. Furthermore, many of the lifesaving preventive treatments for heart disease that were largely tested in men (such as aspirin, statins, and beta-blockers) were not proactively prescribed for women. As a result, the decline of heart disease–related deaths in women has lagged that of men.[65] The failure to understand the manifestations of heart disease in women has resulted in unnecessary health consequences, deaths, and tremendous costs to families, the health-care system, the financial markets, and the economy.

Why did it take decades to understand what heart disease looks like in women? Could dollars and lives have been saved if women had been better represented at the earliest stages when the original heart disease studies were designed? Has the increase in the percentage of female cardiologists in the United States—from 8.9% in 2006 to 14% in 2017—resulted in better-designed research that studies more diverse patient populations?[66]

The scientists who designed the early studies on heart disease were all men, while the composition of the research design team from the Women's Health Initiative was greater than 60% women.[67] While it is impossible to know for sure, it is easy to conclude that the delay and cost to individuals and society could have been minimized if women had been included in the design of the studies from the start. Hopefully, having diverse talent to design medical research projects will prevent more misadventures in the future and grow the pie for healthier and wealthier individuals, families, and society.

Problem-Solving: Put Those Closest to the Problem Closer to Developing the Solution

Near the end of my career at Kaiser Permanente (KP), I (Ruth) served as the medical director at the Care Management Institute (CMI) in the KP national offices. CMI is a shared resource of the Kaiser Health Plan and the Permanente Federation. One of my responsibilities at CMI was to help develop and implement a national performance improvement program that was loosely based on existing models such as Lean Six Sigma and the Toyota Production System.[68] The goal of health-care performance improvement is threefold: improve the quality of care, decrease costs, and elevate the experience ("satisfaction") for patients. KP's performance improvement model is an approach to health-care problem-solving that looks at all aspects of the health-care delivery system—from operating room inventory management, to fixing the referral systems for oncology patients, to preventing patients from having to be readmitted after discharge from the hospital.

While the KP approach was agnostic to the type of problem it could solve, one fundamental aspect of the program was constant—all problem-solving work groups needed to consist of multistakeholder teams. This meant that the people who were closest to the problem were directly involved in creating the solutions. This included the folks who stocked the shelves in the operating room, the medical assistants who did the data entry when a patient was referred to oncology, and the patients themselves. This approach is based on the evidence that frontline workers' innovative solutions improve both the effectiveness and the productivity of a system. In medicine, this translates into better quality, lower costs, and higher satisfaction.[69]

Another fundamental principle of performance improvement in health care is the involvement of patients in the design of research or programs. In the 1980s, when I (Ruth) began my medical career, the notion of including people with a specific disease in the design of a clinical trial to test a new treatment for that disease was radical. Health administrators and doctors had many concerns about dealing with patients who knew little about the science. How would they know about statistics or research design? How could they possibly contribute anything worthwhile to the process? How much work would it take to educate patients to a point where they could contribute to the study design? And on and on.

As it turns out, having people at the table who have experienced the diseases that the scientists are trying to treat is now considered essential by national health bodies such as the United Kingdom's National Institute for Health Research.[70] The people who are closest to the problems are best able to inform the solutions.

Why is this "proximity to problems" important to us? How does it interact with women's financial leadership? Take a look at the most pressing world challenges: health care, unemployment, education, climate refugees, violence. Women are often the group most directly impacted. Solving these problems creates investment opportunities. Consider US health care. As we repeatedly saw in the videos of essential workers leaving their posts in the early days of the pandemic, women make up most of the essential workforce in health care. From nurses to medical assistants to respiratory therapists and physicians, women are the majority. This is true in the United States and even more so around the world. And while men who are infected are more likely to die from COVID-19, women are often the ones taking their husbands/fathers/brothers/grandfathers to the hospital. In normal times, we know that women are the primary consumers of health care and make most of the health-care decisions for their families. Yet women make up less than 35% of hospital system CEOs, less than 10% of pharmaceutical company CEOs and directors, and less than 15% of insurance company CEOs.[71] Only 7–9% of biotech CEOs are women.[72]

Although women make most of the decisions about the individual use of health care, they are not the ones solving problems in the system. The previous discussion of heart disease is a splendid example of the improvements in outcomes that occur when women are involved in health-care research and the allocation of enormous medical research dollars—largely because they are closer to the experience of heart disease as patients, caregivers, and doctors.

Gender-based violence (GBV) is another pressing concern where proximity to the problem can help guide the solutions. It occurs within families and in communities and has a devastating impact on individuals, families, and society at large. The trauma causes both mental and physical hardships, generates enormous health-care costs, and prevents individuals from performing at school or in the workplace, thereby stifling economic growth and development. While people of all genders can be the victims of GBV, the impact is overwhelmingly on women. Many structures in our societies help perpetuate GBV, such as how prosecution of crimes is prioritized, cultural traditions, and the design of cities. One significant opportunity to decrease violence is through better urban planning. Once again, here is a situation where women are the closest to the problems that poorly designed cities can cause, yet traditionally the people who have designed our cities have been men. As Vicki Phillips writes in *Forbes*, "Because urban planning and architecture have long been dominated by men, the reality of how women use and travel through spaces has too often been an afterthought in the design of urban environments, leading to inconveniences (such as small public restrooms) as well as serious dangers (such as low visibility areas) for women. As a result, the geographies of many cities perpetuate gender inequities and violence."[73]

Phillips cites an article from urban planner Jennifer Gardner and design researcher Larissa Begault, who write in *Behavioral Scientist* magazine, "Inequality is spatially reinforced by design, from our systems all the way down to individual public spaces."[74]

What would it look like if women had the opportunity to redesign spaces to combat violence? An interesting experiment took place in Maputo, Mozambique, called the Maputo Safe City Program. Maputo is a city where seven out of ten girls experience violence in public places. Two young women started taking photos of all the areas at their school and neighborhood where they felt unsafe. They shared the photos with their friends and community, which brought the attention of local officials who were able to help make changes, such as relocating the girls' bathrooms and demolishing an abandoned building.[75] Engaging the girls most impacted by the violence in designing the solutions improved the safety of the town for everyone.

Another example of how those who are closest to the problem of urban violence can create innovative solutions happened in New Delhi. Kalpana Viswanath was horrified by the gang rape of a young woman on a city bus in 2012.[76] She saw an urgent need for women to easily identify the level of danger in New Delhi's public spaces, so she created an app called Safetipin.[77] Through crowdsourcing and other methods, this mobile app identifies areas of the city that are unsafe. App users can do a safety audit to evaluate their city and add their own comments. They can report problems that might put all pedestrians at higher risk, such as poor lighting, broken paths, or exposed wiring. Just as a sophisticated GPS app can tell us within seconds where there are speed traps or accidents on highways, the developers of Safetipin have used similar technology to identify where a woman is most at risk of being raped on her way home from work or where there are downed power lines that could cause fires or other injuries.[78] The company's mission is to build a city where women can move around without fear, but the result is a city that's safer and more productive for all. This is another case where women's leadership resulted in a better environment while saving money for everyone. Women need the financial power to direct more capital to these types of solutions.

Now let's consider climate natural disasters and women subsistence farmers. Women are already heavily involved as climate actors. From intimately understanding weather cycles to growing more than 50% of the world's food, to being on the frontlines of climate disaster relief efforts, women are living with climate change in ways that make them the ultimate experts in the field.[79] Underinvestment in these women leaves their entire communities worse off. When they have a platform and capital to fuel their efforts, their climate innovation has boundless potential for economies.

Take, for example, female farmers in Ghana, where women are responsible for 80% of the country's food production. Their small-scale farms are heavily reliant on normal rainfall and consistent weather patterns.[80] The women who farm have deep generational knowledge of fertilizers, crop rotations, natural insecticides, and effective growing seasons.[81] However, their farming efforts are at a subsistence level, focused on feeding their families, not for selling at commercial markets. Hence, their labor is not included in Ghana's GDP. Their work is critical for supporting the Ghanaian economy—because other cash-earning workers are dependent on these crops for sustenance—but it does not have worth in current economic measures. Discounting the labor of these women has had a devastating impact on

Ghana's ability to rebuild following climate crises and on the country's climate-mitigation strategies.

In 2007, a disastrous flood in the north of Ghana killed 57, displaced more than 330,000, and destroyed that year's crop. Greatly exacerbating the economic effect of the crop destruction, however, was the fact that female farmers' labor was ignored by Ghanaian economists in calculating Ghana's GDP. Their lack of economic representation meant that there were no policy measures ready to help them recover from the flood, because Ghana's policies were designed toward those economic actors who, on paper, "make money."[82] These policy gaps forced regions of the country into deeper poverty than the flood itself, as people who relied on these crops now needed to spend larger portions of their limited household budgets buying food. Women farmers were plunged into debt, taking out loans to restart their farms, and children faced malnutrition due to the farms shutting down. It became clear that female subsistence farming is vital for the resilience of the country's economy.[83]

Women like the Ghanaian small-holder farmers are expert climate actors. They must be included in climate policy and investment strategies for their sakes and the sake of their communities, their countries, and the world. Who knows the land better than the people who have grown food on it for generations? Who can see more clearly what we need to do to meet the demands of a changing climate than those who face it every day? Discounting subsistence farming from Ghana's GDP limits the country's capacity to improve its response to climate change and increases the potential of economic catastrophe following natural disasters. If these farmers had the same decision-making power as male farmers, how would they wield it? All evidence strongly suggests they would use their power to combat climate change and teach innovative, sustainable solutions for land management. There is enormous potential for positive change when women are connected to solutions. First, we must redefine what people value as talent and recognize what truly delivers economic upside and then harness and grow this potential.

BENEFITING FROM LEADERSHIP DIFFERENCES

There are inherent differences in how men and women think and lead. When women share in leadership and financial decision-making, there is enhanced performance across multiple dimensions. Research shows that companies employing more women in senior positions are more profitable, more socially responsible, and safer to work for. They also provide higher-quality customer experiences.[84]

But before we get to the detailed evidence to support this position, we offer an explanation. We know that it is not appropriate to generalize about any group of people. The behavior of individuals in any group varies across bell-shaped curves. The last thing we'd want to do in writing this book is to contribute to unhealthy gender stereotyping. Plenty of people who identify as men exhibit characteristics that we are attributing to female leadership, and plenty of people who identify as women have what we would consider to be classic male leadership styles. We also recognize that some differences are due to cultural exposure, not biology. With these disclaimers in mind, this section of the book will look in more detail at the patterns in leadership behavior that provide a rationale for a connection between women's financial decision-making and enhanced outcomes for individuals and economies.

The first factor we consider is that women tend to engage in a collaborative leadership style and are less susceptible to ego-based decision-making. They also engage in diffused or network leadership styles that are less hierarchical than traditional male styles.[85] Additionally, there is convincing evidence that women are less likely to engage in high-risk behavior and take a longer view in their decision-making. They tend to be more empathetic and consider the broader impact of their decisions on the community.[86] Why would these leadership traits result in improved performance, both in social outcomes and financial outcomes? What are the specific actions that women are more likely to take that have this effect?

A study published in *Harvard Business Review* offers insights that may help us understand these specific actions and the impact of these patterns in leadership. The researchers examined 163 multinational companies that had just appointed women to their leadership teams to see whether there were subsequent changes in the companies' strategic approaches.[87] They were able to identify two prominent trends. First, companies became more open to change and less open to risk, as demonstrated by a shift in the language used in communications. The researchers used a standard word categorization methodology and detected a 14% decrease in risk-taking words (such as *bold, venture,* and *chance*) and a 10% increase in the use of words that demonstrated openness to change (such as *create, transform,* and *launch*). Second, the companies experienced a decreased emphasis on mergers and acquisitions and an increased emphasis on research and development (R&D) resulting in, on average, a 1.1% increase in R&D budgets. This trend is consistent with other evidence that strongly suggests women are more likely to invest in the long-term health and sustainability of companies rather than seek short-term profits. This study gives us some insights into the specific behaviors that are demonstrated by collaborative, network-focused leaders that contribute to healthier and wealthier companies.[88]

As we will discuss in chapter 3, we are living through a time of disruption and dislocation. Throughout the world, economies have shifted from subsistence farming to manufacturing and from manufacturing to service delivery. These changing circumstances require collaboration, networking, and long-view leadership skills that so many women can offer. We believe that everyone can be more collaborative and, in fact, must be to take full advantage of today's business and governance opportunities. Through an inclusive, total talent paradigm, we will all be healthier and wealthier.

Collaborative Leadership

Let us look at some examples of the impact of women's leadership styles in more detail. In her book *Collaboration Code*, Carol Mitchell describes how women are more likely to exhibit leadership styles that are empathetic, communicative, cautious, and focused on the long term while being less driven by personal ego.[89] The COVID-19 pandemic is one of the defining aspects of our time, and it shows how female leadership during the period of our analysis has paid off. As the COVID-19 pandemic launched into every corner of the world, countries with female leaders—New Zealand, Finland, Iceland, and Germany—exhibited differences in how they managed through the crisis when compared to countries with male leaders. These female leaders took a long view of the dislocation the world was facing, which resulted in a positive impact on their economies and their citizens. Aside from adoption of cautious preventive measures, including closing borders and implementing lockdowns, they were able to communicate to their citizenry the importance of strong contact tracing and testing programs, quarantining, and travel restrictions.[90] These women leaders also pushed for similar social policies and economic stimulus and displayed similar leadership behaviors despite the cultural differences among their respective countries.

Critically important was consistent and empathetic communication. In spring 2020, Finland's Interior Minister Maria Ohisalo reflected on gender differences in *Forbes:* "Something that I've noticed . . . many male leaders were focusing on the economical aspect quite a lot. While we focused on the idea that we are protecting you . . . the health of everybody here . . . (W)ould it be easier for a female leader to take this into the core of all the politics that we are actually protecting the human life?"[91]

Prime Minister Jacinda Ardern of New Zealand went so far as to livestream COVID-19–related announcements from her own home, where she was able to show that she, too, was a mother learning to cope with a new way of managing her own family through the crisis.[92] Her proposals for social and economic policies were more compelling as

they were based on a personal understanding of citizens'
needs. Ardern recognized early on that giving families the
support they needed to transition to home-based work was
important to the country's virus-containment strategy. New
Zealand's fiscal support packages, among the largest in the
world relative to the size of the country's economy, included
wage subsidies to help workers keep their jobs. This strategy
enabled businesses to reopen quickly and effectively as lockdowns ended—without having to lay off workers, provide
them with unemployment, then rehire them again, which
would have been a less efficient way to manage through the
economic crisis that followed the health crisis.[93]

Prime Minister Katrín Jakobsdóttir of Iceland prioritized allowing women to stay in the workforce. She recognized that women were critical workers in the infrastructure
that was helping the country manage the crisis, including
the health-care, welfare, and early- and late-age care
systems. Her government's efforts focused on reopening
schools as early as possible; schools in Iceland were open by
August 2020.[94]

The early successes of these female-led countries mitigated the impacts of the economic crises that impacted
too many other countries: a 2021 IMF report ranked
New Zealand fourth among Organization for Economic
Co-operation and Development (OECD) countries in
terms of economic recovery in late 2020 and reported
the country was on track for 4% real GDP growth by
May 2021.[95]

In spring 2020, Finland's Prime Minister Sanna
Marin acted promptly and slowed the spread of the
virus.[96] The OECD reported that Finland's economy

during the early stages of COVID was less negatively impacted than they had forecast, and that "(t)he Finnish government's effective crisis management ha(d) mitigated the shocks."[97]

Iceland's tourism industry fully reopened; the OECD projected GDP growth of 2.8% in 2021 and 4.7% in 2022.[98] And Germany, caught directly in the heart of the European outbreak zone, still managed to outperform most of Europe. It minimized its economic contraction in 2020 and forecasted 3.6% GDP growth for 2021.[99]

In the early months of the pandemic, the countries with female-led governments had fewer cases and fewer deaths when compared to the United States.[100] We recognize that these statistics represent isolated cases drawn from publicly available data. We do not mean to draw causation where there may be none. However, we can review the policies implemented and behaviors exhibited by these women leaders and how they inspired good behavior and public unity from their citizens and then think about the potential opportunity of female leadership to weathering the crises yet to come. Will millions of lives and billions of dollars be saved if there are more women serving as national leaders in the future? We say yes, and there's data to support our assertion.

For other evidence of women's collaborative leadership style in government, we can examine the literature on women and men in parliaments. In 2008, the Inter-Parliamentary Union (IPU) published the findings of its comprehensive survey of 272 parliamentarians in 110 countries across the globe. The survey included personal interviews with 20 parliamentarians. Of note, 40% of the respondents were men. The survey questions specifically addressed women's contributions to decision-making. In regard to leadership styles, the study found that "two thirds of respondents believed that women's caucuses have been successful in uniting women across party lines."[101] This study also found that two-thirds of the respondents (including 63% of the male respondents) "did not think the presence of women was sufficient" on their committees.[102]

The positive impact of women's leadership styles can be seen in the race to create COVID-19 vaccines. As we look at how the world has been able to start emerging from a near crippling crisis in a relatively brief time, we must focus on the vaccines and the roles women played in their development. Having a vaccine for a virus that was discovered less than a year before is truly a miracle. However, the real story of the vaccine development is one of immense patience, hard work, and dedication from female scientists.

In 1985, Dr. Katalin Karikó stuffed £900 into a teddy bear, scooped up her infant daughter, and emigrated with her husband from Hungary to the United States. She had been offered a grant at the University of Pennsylvania to study mRNA.[103] Although that move should have been the start of endless opportunities, when she got to Pennsylvania she found that her grant requests were consistently refused as her research was deemed "too novel." In this chapter we are making the point that female leaders are less driven by ego and immediate results, and Dr. Karikó is a prime example. Instead of being deterred by numerous refusals, instead of packing in her mRNA research and choosing to study something more mainstream or something she knew she'd be noticed for, she continued to focus on her mRNA work. She took a long view and understood the research's potential. In the thirty-five years between her emigration and the COVID-19 pandemic, Dr. Karikó worked tirelessly on mRNA, making many discoveries. Even after her own bioresearch company, cofounded with Dr. Drew Weissman, could not acquire enough grant money to get off the ground, Dr. Karikó remained steadfast in her pursuit. She was eventually hired by BioNTech, a vaccine company that later merged with Pfizer. In 2020, the world finally heard about her and how her mRNA expertise was critical to engineering both the Pfizer and Moderna COVID-19 vaccines. In her April 2021 *New York Times* article, "Kati Kariko Helped Shield the World from Coronavirus," Gina Kolata quotes Dr. Anthony Fauci as saying of this mRNA research: "It's going to be transforming. It is already transforming for Covid-19, but also for other vaccines. H.I.V.—people in the field are already excited. Influenza, malaria."[104]

Another scientist who was instrumental in the search for the vaccine is Dr. Sarah Gilbert of Oxford University. She used her years of experience in vaccine development to create AstraZeneca's COVID-19 vaccine. Dr. Gilbert is another example of someone who had been working in the field for decades without high-profile recognition. In a write-up about the development of the vaccine, colleagues acknowledged that the quick turnaround was due in part to Dr. Gilbert's dedication to teamwork and collaboration within her lab, making it a place where people felt driven to do their best work.[105]

Dr. Kizzmekia Corbett, another female scientist, collaborated on the formulation of the Moderna vaccine.

She also lent her credibility as a Black scientist to encourage Black Americans to have faith in the vaccine; many people were justifiably reluctant to receive it given the history of racist medical trials and treatment in the United States.[106] When the vaccine became widely available in January 2021, surveys showed that 34% of the US's Black population expressed hesitancy about receiving it.[107] Corbett's presence in the lab and her voice in communicating the efficacy of the vaccine will continue to be important if the United States is to vaccinate as many people as possible. Dr. Corbett has been using her expertise as a researcher on the Moderna vaccine to educate others within the Black community. Through all the media at her disposal—church meetings, town halls, Twitter (@KizzyPHD), Instagram live videos, and interviews—she has created a space for open discussion for questions, queries, and anxieties to be answered.[108] From January to March 2021, hesitancy within the Black community regarding the vaccine fell from 34% to 18%; Dr. Corbett has been one of the critical voices in that shift.[109]

Other female scientists also deserve credit. The science around mRNA is based on the lifelong research of Jennifer Doudna and the crucial element of CRISPR gene-editing software, for which she was awarded the 2020 Nobel Prize in Chemistry along with fellow scientist Emmanuelle Charpentier. Although CRISPR can slice up DNA, it uses RNA as a guide to enter the mutating DNA. Dr. Doudna's intense research into RNA and its functioning helped develop a path forward for more RNA and mRNA studies. This guided scientists to ask whether manipulating mRNA could be the key to inoculating people from coronaviruses like COVID-19. Without Charpentier and Doudna's initial research into DNA and RNA, it is unlikely we would have discovered such effective COVID-19 vaccines so quickly.[110]

The stories of these women scientists prompt us to ask why we hear so few stories about them and their work and why it took so long for us to hear about them at all. When we hear stories of scientists such as Dr. Karikó, we should be concerned about bias in capital allocation by grantmakers into research and development and by venture capitalists into translation and commercialization. If Dr. Karikó had received adequate grant funding, if her efforts at commercializing her scientific discoveries had been backed by investors, would the world have had COVID-19 vaccines even earlier in the pandemic? We should all be grateful that Dr. Karikó had the presence of mind and lack of ego to make mRNA research her life's work despite such rejections. But we should also keep in mind that there may be dozens of Katalin Karikós out there, working in labs across the world, their efforts stymied as they are denied research money. For their sake, and ours, we need to remodel our grant and capital allocation systems to enable female researchers to access the funding they need for their projects.

There may be hope in the fact that Dr. Derrick Rossi, the Canadian cell biologist who founded Moderna, is pushing to have Dr. Karikó's work finally recognized. In 2005, Dr. Rossi read one of Dr. Karikó's papers on mRNA and became so fascinated by her research that he procured financial backers for his own biotech company with the intention of using mRNA in his own inventions. While Dr. Karikó faced endless financial barriers to support her research, Dr. Rossi was able to get funding and founded his company, Moderna, in Cambridge, Massachusetts, in 2010.

He eventually used mRNA as the blueprint for Moderna's COVID-19 vaccine. He is now petitioning for Dr. Karikó to win the Nobel Prize.[111]

These examples from the history of COVID-19 vaccine development demonstrate how technological innovations transform the world every day, keeping us safe and growing economies. By including female talent in these advancements, we witness the effects of women's collaborative leadership.

Portugal is an example of applying the female characteristics of collaborative leadership to national technological ambitions with significant social and economic impact. Over the past fifteen years, Portugal has transformed itself with the hope of becoming a technology hub in Europe. The country has created the foundational infrastructure to be successful.[112] Many women have been instrumental in Portugal's push toward technological leadership, including Maria Manuel Leitão Marques as minister of the presidency and administrative modernization and Graça Fonseca as the secretary of state between 2015 and 2018.[113]

The government program, named Simplex, uses a citizen-centric approach with a strong focus on collaboration. Their key innovation was a multiyear de-bureaucratization initiative based around the ideas that government should be agile; public services should be accessible, seamless, and efficient; and regulatory burdens should be minimal. The program has been and continues to be led by women, prioritizes consultations with citizens and the civil service workforce, and requires administrators to set annual targets based on these consultations with the end users. This user-centered, collaborative process requires commitment to embrace complexity in the short term as the government had to establish the infrastructure for such consultations. Overall, it has worked to Portugal's social and economic advantage, with technology companies and other remote workforces moving to the country and driving a rebound in economic growth after Portugal's recession of 2007–2008. The country has successfully recruited tech companies such as Uber to set up shop and invest over 90 million euros in Lisbon. As Anabel Diaz, regional general director at Uber, was quoted in the *Portugal News*, "Since we arrived seven years ago, the Portuguese market has been a hub of innovation and growth where we were able to create and test products such as Uber Green or the expansion of the service to 100 percent of the territory, among many other innovative projects and initiatives."[114]

The Simplex approach has led to fifteen hundred changes that improve the design and delivery of digital services, including projects such as the creation of a one-stop online portal to sign up for public services and the implementation of more "citizen kiosks" where people can sign up for services in person when preferred. The Portuguese justice ministry, also led by women, has seen similar innovation.[115] Key projects such as *Justiça+próxima*, designed to simplify the administration of justice and bring it closer to citizens' lives, along with the push for integrated service centers, digitization of individual identification, and a government interoperability platform, have won Portugal recognition from the OECD as best in class in the region.[116] Overall, the greatest gain from this collaborative leadership might be how it brought a culture of innovation to government, which is often regarded as slow and clumsy in the face of change.

Most conversations about women and technology have focused on the limited number of women in the scientific and engineering fields. What if, in addition to encouraging more women to enter these fields of study, we also made it a priority to leverage the different leadership skills of women already in these fields? In the case study of Portugal, the country invited women technologists to develop the platforms and infrastructure that is powering positive change and accelerating the pace of economic growth. Instead of dismissing women as absent or badly represented in the tech world, we should be asking how much stronger and more user-friendly our tech capacity would be if more female talent were engaged and more women had leadership roles in innovation, capital allocation, and more.

Network and Diffused Leadership

The leadership that will be essential to meet our new environmental and social challenges is one that relies on networks, decentralized or "diffused" influence, and tempering of egos. This style is also more common among women. Network leadership provides groups with guidelines, then allows them freedom and flexibility to customize solutions to their communities. In a recent podcast, Malcolm Gladwell described network leadership as the leadership style likely to become more prevalent in our post-pandemic world.[117] He concedes that network leadership can be messy and less efficient to start but asserts that it can yield better results in the medium and longer terms by including diverse input in innovations.

The pandemic period has allowed us a window into how effective and positive network leadership can be and how women are quite good at it. In the case of developing the COVID-19 vaccines, scientists, a considerable number of whom were female, collaborated across labs and private companies. Even having just a few women in a leadership group can significantly alter the work style and culture. We are all better off for that network collaboration. Instead of the lack of cooperation or transparency that is typical in the competitive world of drug development, COVID-19 vaccines development were accelerated and resulted in products in record time.

Another area where network leadership paid off was the response of the Black Lives Matter (BLM) movement after the killing of Mr. George Floyd. BLM had been founded by three relatively unknown women, Alicia Garza, Patrisse Cullors, and Opal Tometi.[118] They provided a national blueprint, and then communities went on to develop their local strategies. This is different from the historical civil rights movement of the 1960s, in which Dr. Martin Luther King Jr. was the central and relatively hierarchical leader. Notably, having a single leader also meant that targeting him would put the organizational apparatus at risk. Diffused leadership mitigates against key person risk—if one leader is not available, the organization still functions relatively well.

Another clear case of network leadership is the Fridays for Future climate strikes inspired by Greta Thunberg's School Strikes for Climate, which have been going on since she first started protesting outside of the Swedish parliament in 2018. Now people of all genders all over the world are following her lead. Although her strikes were the impetus for a larger movement, social media—in this case used positively—enabled her protests to go viral, inspiring other climate activists around the world to start their own strikes. Now anybody can go to the Fridays for Future website to find a protest near them or to plan one themselves. The protests have also reached beyond marches. Young climate activists are getting involved in policy debates, pushbacks, and idea generation.[119]

Fridays for Future is a collectivist movement. Climate change is a global issue so it makes little sense to have one leader in one location leading the struggle. The movement needs a highly networked, collectivist mindset and many frontline leaders to grapple with local disasters. Additionally, Fridays for Future campaigners argue that the climate situation has gotten as bad as it currently is in part *because of* the hierarchical leadership structures that are currently the norm. To beat back climate change, we need as many voices leading the way as possible.

Why would women thrive in network or diffused leadership roles? Perhaps women prefer to exhibit network leadership because they are often a minority in rooms of power and maneuvering in these spaces is easier with allies rather than on their own. Whatever the answer is, the next economy will be better served by diffused leadership, especially if coupled with a long view. As Malcolm Gladwell said in *Inc.* about the strengths and weaknesses of hierarchical leadership versus network leadership, "The important question is, which of these two models is winning? . . . What I think has happened with the pandemic is, the network has won. What we are going to take away from this experience is a clear preference for that way of organizing ourselves over the old one."[120]

Risk Awareness and the Long View

Countless studies have shown that women tend to take fewer dangerous risks than men. This could come from a combination of greater cautiousness and decreased susceptibility to competitive machismo behaviors. Women are more risk-aware and less likely to make unnecessary risky choices. In our current era of boom-and-bust economies, we could all benefit from leaders who are less likely to bet everything on a new trend without looking at long-term considerations.

A recent *Forbes* article noted, "Studies show that women spend more time researching their investment choices. And while they do take on less risk than men when it comes to investing, that doesn't mean they're risk averse. Rather, they're simply more risk aware, likely to take on appropriate levels of risk with their investments than men. Both of these findings make for better investing outcomes."[121] Some have proposed that women mitigate men's overconfidence.[122] Outside of financial decision-making, there's evidence that women are more risk-conscious and less likely to gamble. They are more likely to avoid conflict, seek general consensus, and stay the course through difficult transformations.[123]

In examples from the world of gambling we see a clear difference between men and women. While men are more likely to gamble for social reasons, women are more likely to gamble either for charity or to distract themselves from daily stress.[124] Because men gamble more often in social settings, it could explain why they take bigger risks, as this social context sets men up for competitive risk encouragement. Women, on the other hand, do not want to lose money for the charity they're gambling for or add to their stress by having a risky move fail to pay off. In addition, when women find themselves on a gambling binge, they are more open to seeking help. One study from Australia found that 40.5% of women with problem gambling reported seeking help to manage it compared to only 18% of affected men.[125] This illustrates further that women are more cautious about risk-taking and likely more proactive about trying to stop it in its tracks. Men are more likely to expect a positive outcome from a gambling risk, whereas women are more likely to expect the worst. Men encourage other men to take higher risks for social capital when gambling, whereas women don't appear to apply this type of pressure to one another.[126] It is impossible to tell whether these different perceptions of risk are based on inherent biological or socialized differences, but regardless of the cause, they are critical. They suggest that women will take fewer risks and weigh potential losses, whereas men may be more cavalier with their gambling because they focus on potential gains rather than the downsides. We should acknowledge that depending on the context, a certain amount of risk-taking is beneficial but excessive risk-taking can be negative. The best scenario is when the decision-makers are aware of the risks and can make educated decisions based on a diversity of input.

Leaving the casino and entering the boardroom, we see that women have a direct impact on the risk-taking behavior of the boards they are on. As with gambling behavior, women in boardrooms don't influence their male codirectors to make risky decisions.[127] This helps to further illustrate how women are less susceptible to machismo culture and, in fact, temper it.

A study from Indonesia found the same pattern as the study of US-based company boards—more women on the board lowered the company's overall risk.[128] *Harvard Business Review*'s collection of research on women in C-suites adds more evidence. When women are a part of decision-making, they encourage companies to embrace change while simultaneously lowering risk-taking.[129] Additionally, women not only bring innovative ideas but encourage a shift in thinking within the organizations by their presence. Companies that added women to the C-suite showed a dramatic shift in energy and resources from acquisitions (a "knowledge buying" approach) to research and development (a "knowledge building" approach). We see again how women tend to embrace longer-term thinking and future-aware strategies rather than short-term gains.

Studies have also shown that women in leadership positions are able to prioritize long-term strategy above short-term gain. Nowhere is this clearer than in the fight against climate change, the current chronic strain on our planet. It takes long-term planning and foresight to understand the risks that human-made ecological harm pose as well as to think ahead about solutions to problems that are lurking on the horizon. Two exemplary long-term ecological thinkers are Dr. Jean Rodgers and the late Rachel Carson.

In 1945, Monsanto won the Nobel Prize for the contribution made to the Vietnam War from their pesticide DDT. At the time, malaria carried by mosquitoes harmed American military members stationed in the Pacific Islands. DDT was so effective it wiped out the malaria-carrying mosquitos on the Pacific Islands. Following the war, the bug spray was released for public use with the promise of pest-free land for farmers who embraced DDT. But a handful of naturalists, including Rachel Carson, suspected that such a far-reaching pesticide could have unintended consequences for the food chain.[130]

Ten years later, DDT was massively popular across the United States and Europe. At the same time, dead birds were starting to fall from trees. People were reporting that the birds now had brittle eggshells and that the fish in streams appeared to be sickly. Nobody suspected that the prevalence of DDT could have contributed to the wildlife degradation. Nobody except Rachel Carson. In her paradigm-shifting book *Silent Spring*, Carson lays out in clear detail exactly how this human-made pesticide had seeped into the food chain, poisoning fish, mammals, and, infamously, baby birds. Carson held on to her initial skepticism for thirteen years, never ceasing to question the expansive effects of DDT, and was able to channel her long-term thinking into her studies, resulting in the publication of the era's most influential book on environmentalism.[131]

When Carson released the book, she was subject to defamatory abuse. As reported in 2017 in the *Saturday Evening Post*, Edwin Diamond, a senior editor at *Newsweek* who reviewed the book in 1963, was quoted as saying, "her arguments were more emotional than accurate" and called it the work of an era of "shrill voices."[132] A review in *TIME* magazine used the words *witchy* and *hysterical* to describe Carson. Monsanto attacked her by questioning everything from her scientific knowledge to her sanity.[133] However, Monsanto's attempts to silence Carson were ultimately ineffective. The EPA banned DDT in 1972 "based on its adverse environmental effects, such as those to wildlife, as well as its potential human health risks."[134]

Many now consider *Silent Spring* to be the book that launched the modern environmental movement because it opened the gates for people to question and criticize corporations and inventions. Before its publication, few people wondered whether human-made creations could affect the natural world. But Carson proved this was happening in deeply alarming ways. *Silent Spring* demonstrated the negative impact from large industries that prioritize profit over longer-term vision, environmental planning, and planetary ethics. The book's success and impact showed burgeoning environmentalists that their efforts could make a real difference.

It took someone with an ability to be concerned about the long-term effects of a product, not just its short-term gain, to raise the alarm bells on DDT. Carson was unafraid of industry backlash and was meticulous in her research and preparedness. She exhibited so many of the characteristics that we see attributed to female leaders: less ego-driven decision-making, long-term vision over short-term gain, curiosity, healthy skepticism, the ability to listen, and, in her case, the patience and ability to collect vast amounts of evidence from people around the country and across the Atlantic.

Dr. Jean Rodgers showed this same level of long-term thinking when she created the Sustainability Accounting Standards Board (SASB).[135] In 2011, Dr. Rodgers saw that there was an emerging market for sustainability but there was no corporate framework to use when discussing it. People wanted to start investing in the environment, or in women, or in other social impact fields, but there was no universal standard to measure the sustainable worth or positive force of an investment. Dr. Rodgers recognized that the core definition of long-term profitability in the twenty-first century cannot be moneymaking alone. Businesses also need to have data security, promote climate sustainability, and manage conflicts of interest.

She realized there was no language to measure success in areas beyond pure profit-making. So she created the SASB, which offers 77 standards for industries to use to determine the efficacy of their sustainability practices. What differentiates SASB from other impact framework organizations is that SASB focuses on tangible, replicable standards. It sets metrics and industry-specific goals that companies can measure themselves against. The detail-oriented nature of Dr. Rodgers's leadership has made meeting sustainable goals easier for companies that want to do good and whose leaders recognize that the future of corporate business is inextricably linked with sustainability goals. Being a company with positive-impact goals is fine, but these goals don't mean much if there are no metrics by which to measure progress. SASB exists to provide standards that turn the theoretical potential of impact organizations into something concrete.

The work of women, especially Black women, in the field of artificial intelligence (AI) technologies is another demonstration of long-term thinking. In January 2020, someone in Detroit stole a Shinola watch worth $3,800. The police on the scene went through their usual routine of reviewing the security cameras, but this time they had AI-powered facial recognition software to help identify the grainy face of a Black man on the screen. The algorithm gave them a facial match, and they drove to the suburbs and arrested the man whose image was shown on the computer screen in front of his wife and children. The police had followed all the steps, complied with the algorithm, and completed an arrest. The only issue was, they had the wrong man. The algorithm could not differentiate between features on darker-skinned people.[136]

This is just one example of many incidents where AI software has failed to correctly identify the face of a person of color. A study done on the five most widely used facial recognition programs—Microsoft, Face++, IBM, Amazon, and Kairos—found that every one of them was much less likely to correctly identify the face of a darker-skinned woman compared to a darker-skinned man, or lighter-skinned men and women.[137] If we are entering an age where the police rely on facial recognition to make arrests, or where people use AI to enter buildings, or to use their phones, or to accomplish any other everyday task, then it is imperative that these systems do not have built-in biases.

One group on the front lines of the fight against this bias is the Algorithmic Justice League (AJL), created by three women whose mission is to illuminate the problematic biases in AI. Their website's motto is "We want the world to remember that who codes matter, how we code matters, and that we can code a better future."[138] Founder Joy Buolamwini wrote her MIT thesis on uncovering gender and racial bias in AI. The dramatic gap in AI's capabilities disturbed her so much that she launched AJL to promote research and advocacy in the field of AI bias.

The need for people concerned about AI to form their own advocacy groups became even more apparent when Timnit Gebru, one of Google's AI leaders, was fired after she wrote and published a paper criticizing Google's AI language for being too centered on Western languages and for being unable to adapt to different languages and cultures.[139] Gebru is an advisor for the group Black in AI, an organization that centers the knowledge of Black people in the artificial intelligence space. The relative lack of Black programmers creating AI applications such as facial recognition software has had deeply damaging effects on the Black community. Black in AI hopes to reduce biases in the field by having Black programmers build applications that reflect them and, by extension, the wider world. When innovative technologies emerge with the potential to solve complicated problems, it's important to have systems and platforms in place to watch out for inadvertent biases and harm that might be caused by the technologies. This is where organizations such as AJL come in. Created by concerned program-mers—in AJL's case, all women—they support one another's research integrity instead of just promoting a product. Overall, this approach will make AI-run prod-ucts better and safer and more trustworthy for all who use them or are subject to their use.

Ironically, Gebru had been hired specifically because of her expertise in AI biases to help Google address the compa-ny's lack of diversity. She was fired when she identified and pushed back against their practices.

We need long-view thinkers in the AI world who see the potential benefits of software as well as the drawbacks. We need people who can see beyond the hype and excitement surrounding innovative technologies, who can perceive and call out the dangers these technologies pose to communities, especially people from communities that often are not involved in the development process or do not have a platform to voice their concerns. It is not surprising that the leaders in this research are women given everything that we see about women having an affinity for long-term thinking. If AI-enabled software is our future, investors will need to identify companies that are including diverse innovators to address potential harm at the product development phase. These safeguards will protect us all from biased AI.

A Bell-Shaped Curve

We have used evidence to demonstrate that women are excellent financial decision-makers. When they are in control of capital, there will be better overall results for individuals, communities, and economies. But there are no absolutes when it comes to human behavior.

Most leaders simultaneously exhibit some typically female and some typically male leadership qualities. Consider, for instance, the first female British prime minister, Margaret Thatcher, first referred to as the "Iron Lady" in the Soviet Union's press. She set the stage for her tough leadership when she came into power and broke the coal unions' grip on the British economy.[140] As much as she was not considered an empathetic leader, she had the long view. That was part of how she was able to break the union members' will so that the miners returned to work without the government making any concessions. She took advance action, stockpiling coal and making side deals with non-union drivers so the country would still be able to produce power when the unionized miners were on strike. This was the first big step in her efforts to change the British economy into one that was more individualistic and capitalistic. Thatcher changed her country by conforming to a more male model of leadership. For example, to be taken more seriously, she reportedly had voice lessons to make her voice sound deeper and more "masculine." She had an autocratic style of governance—she was not a consensus builder or a team player in any way.[141] She led by her own opinions and was not known for working well with others. We wonder if Thatcher's success in breaking down the unions was partly because her opponents might have underestimated her strength. We also wonder whether shutting down an industry without plans for other economic activities to absorb the workforce and grow the pie was shortsighted. Might a more empathetic leader have been both strong in loosening the grip of unions on the economy and equally determined to create new industries to absorb the affected workforce?

The prevalence of human behaviors tends to follow a bell-shaped curve. Some women will not exhibit the characteristics we have described in this chapter; most women will be in the middle, and then there will be women who exhibit these gender characteristics at significant levels. Individuals exhibit behaviors along a spectrum from more masculine to more feminine. Researchers have studied this spectrum. Without making any judgment about the applicability of the research, we will discuss two studies in this section. One study has broken down the variation in these behaviors into two categories: empathizing and systemizing or analyzing. Simon Baron-Cohen, a clinical psychologist at Cambridge University, has published research indicating that women have more empathizing energy, while men have a more systemizing brain, meaning they enjoy breaking down and analyzing things. According to Baron-Cohen's research, 44% of women have empathizing brains, 17% of women have systemizing brains, and 35% of women have brains that are roughly balanced between the two poles. So far as men are concerned, Baron-Cohen found that 53% of men have systemizing brains, 17% have empathizing brains, and 24% are roughly balanced. The remaining 6% have an extreme male brain, meaning they are highly analytical but lack empathy for others.[142] Additional research supporting the basic thesis that gender characteristics are on a spectrum was published by Professor Daphna Joel, indicating that 8% of people are on the extreme masculine or feminine ends of the spectrum, while the rest of the world's population lies somewhere in the middle.[143]

Throughout history there are many examples of male leaders who exhibit the traits we've described as more typically female, and there are plenty of examples of female leaders who exhibit typical male qualities. However, this variation in behavior doesn't diminish the benefits of gender diversity in financial leadership.

THE BOTTOM LINE

Female talent is vastly underutilized, and women are closer to the problems that need to be solved. Companies with women financial leaders enjoy success in risk mitigation, innovation, and long-term financial performance. Women-led countries do better managing crises. Is this because of the qualities inherent in women leaders or because entities that are more successful are more comfortable with women leaders? Unfortunately, since we cannot start the human experiment from scratch with a randomized trial, we need to rely on observational data that shows successes as new types of challenges emerge. We see many examples, including national leadership during the pandemic, vaccine development, climate change, and new civil rights movements, which demonstrate that women-led organizations are well suited to managing these challenges. It is not our intent to argue for causation or correlation. Rather, it is to illuminate patterns of behavior across many different situations—from leading a country, to running a company, to nurturing a family. Women tend to exhibit characteristics that drive positive social and financial outcomes. As we will see in the next chapters, these characteristics lead to outcomes that are demonstrably good for society, for economies, for investors, and for all of us, men and women alike.

CHAPTER 2

THE PERFORMANCE EDGE

IMPROVING RETURNS, MANAGING RISK, AND DELIVERING IMPACT

A S INVESTORS, WE HAVE A RESPONSIBILITY TO MANAGE risk and deliver returns. By not including women in investment decisions, are we leaving money on the table?

Gender-focused investing started decades ago as a feminist strategy to empower women. We now know that it generates superior financial returns. Public companies with at least four women on their boards significantly outperform those without. Fortune 500 firms with female board members have better financial performance across multiple indicators. Companies in the top 25% of gender-diverse executive teams were significantly more likely to outperform peers in terms of profitability and value creation. Yet according to a 2020 report from Equileap (an organization that you'll read more about later), among the S&P 500 only 6% of companies have a female CEO, 13% have a female chief financial officer (CFO), and 4% have a female chair.[144] Only four companies (1%) have both a female CEO and CFO: Gap, Arista Networks, Accenture, and Kohl's. Almost 80% of the companies have no women at the chair of the board, CEO, or CFO level.[145] One strategic intervention that would help a public company significantly outperform its competition would be to hire women leaders, so why is this such a well-kept secret?

This direct correlation between female financial decision-making and financial performance extends across all asset classes. Women fund managers, corporate executives, landowners, and debtholders all provide investors with higher returns than do men in these positions.[146] Gender-specific financial performance data, including the robust performance of gender-diverse asset management teams, founders' teams, boards, and corporate management teams, is becoming more available and are showing consistent outperformance by teams that include women. In this section we will review the evidence and discuss the woeful numbers that show the funding and recruitment gap that prevents women's talents from optimizing the next economy.

This book is not intended to engage in a battle of the sexes or even to make the case for all-female teams outperforming all-male teams. Our approach is to evaluate the financial performance of gender-diverse leadership compared to male-only leadership. We demonstrate that if women are excluded from financial decision-making, value is left on the table. This is bad for the growth of investment portfolios and the overall economy. When I (Patience) first started focusing my investment skills on investing in and through women, there was a dearth of such data. The refrain I heard the most was that male CEOs and investors wanted to understand "the business case" for investing in female talent and companies. The post-2008 financial crisis period started changing minds, as those who looked noticed the emerging data indicating that public companies with gender-diverse boards and management teams were on average performing better. Compared to companies with nondiverse boards, their earnings and share prices were more stable, and they were emerging from the depths of the crisis more quickly. Asset managers with gender-diverse teams were faring better with lower overall losses. These companies were not just onboarding women into these positions during the crisis period; instead, they valued diversity as a business practice. These companies had the human infrastructure for managing through market up-and-down cycles and in the long term proved to be more resilient and profitable.

The lessons from that period encouraged me, as I was investing in financial institutions across emerging markets at the time, to start questioning how much of these institutions' capital was being invested in women entrepreneurs. The answer? Not very much. The best regions had allocations in the low 20 percentage points of the total portfolio. A 2011 McKinsey research report commissioned by the IFC identified a global gap of about $300 billion per year between how much funding women entrepreneurs received and the funding they needed.[147] I and my colleagues visited financial institutions in Australia, the United Kingdom, and Nigeria. We saw that female credit portfolios had on average fewer nonperforming loans (NPLs), and banks were on average making slightly more in fees from female clients. The team's review of data indicated that women tended to be loyal clients who fulfilled most of their banking needs with their chosen banker, thereby generating greater fees. I saw an opportunity to build a new business as well as close a financing gap. I started the Banking on Women investment business for the International Finance Corporation. Others around the world were noticing the same type of opportunities. Since then, increasing evidence has been gathered about gender-diverse teams showing strong financial and impact returns.

Unfortunately, despite this early momentum and continued evidence of impressive performance, we have seen limited movement in investments in and through women. Ruth founded the Tara Health Foundation with the bold commitment to invest 100% of the assets of the foundation to support its mission to improve the lives of women and girls. Even more boldly, the investment team received the mandate to be 100% mission-aligned without compromising on financial returns. To accomplish this, the foundation worked with two female investment advisors from Merrill who had already proven themselves to be phenomenal financial analysts and had histories of consistent above-market performance. They leaped at the opportunity to take on the gender-focused investment strategy and build their expertise.

They used a framework called the XX Factor developed by the Center for High Impact Philanthropy at the University of Pennsylvania, which defines the social determinants that are beneficial for women and girls and identifies which investments fit the criteria of being 100% mission-aligned.[148] These five determinants include health, education, economic empowerment, personal safety, and legal rights. If an investment has a social benefit that directly or indirectly impacts one of these five areas, it is included. Eventually, the two female investment advisors added the Invest Your Values tools from As You Sow to further shape their inclusive and exclusive strategies.[149] (As You Sow is a nonprofit that promotes social corporate responsibility through shareholder advocacy and coalition building.)

The Merrill advisors brought their excellent market analysis skills to the table. Rather than seeing the guidelines as constraints, they saw them as opportunities. As a result, after seven years of managing Tara Health Foundation's investment portfolio, they have succeeded in consistently generating well above market performance every year—not *in spite of* being 100% mission-aligned, but *because* they are 100% mission-aligned. Their experience has shown that screening all investments in a diversified portfolio with a gender lens can result in superlative financial returns. Let's take a deeper dive into why Tara Health Foundation and Ruth's personal investment experience is backed up with evidence.

ASSET OWNERS

Women are coming into increasing wealth through their successful companies and inheritance. As asset owners, they have different investment approaches that capital managers who take a long-term perspective must consider. After all, investment choices drive portfolio performance. The Tara Health Foundation's strong portfolio performance discussed above shows that investment portfolios based on the characteristics of women and the choices they make about who manages their wealth and how it is managed will generate strong returns.

What are the different sensibilities of women asset owners? UBS interviewed forty female billionaires and produced a profile of their perspectives on their wealth and the positive impact it could have on economic and social well-being. These 40 women exhibit similar characteristics—humility or low ego (working under the radar), the long view (using their capital to build systems for change), and care for people and the planet (directing their resources to preservation through environmental and social investments). The key takeaways from the conversations with these forty women were that they prioritized investing their wealth in ways that would produce a positive and lasting impact on families, businesses, and society. These women view legacy as using their money to drive lasting change rather than merely making more money and passing it to the next generation.[150] As it turns out, the types of investments that are likely to produce positive and lasting impact are also more likely to create strong financial returns.

One reason these women asset-owners are an important segment of society is that they are an ever-increasing market force as investors. According to the Boston Consulting Group, women were projected to hold $72 trillion in private wealth by 2020, 20% of 2019's total global wealth of $360 trillion.[151] In addition, in the years after 2019, women's wealth is expected to increase at an accelerated rate, adding $5 trillion each year to global wealth.[152] The UBS report goes further, positing that the female billionaires' views coalesce around six approaches to the impact they and their capital can have: creating new structures and approaches, fighting for causes that matter to them, curating and building networks to collaborate with them, preservation of valuable cultural and environmental assets, researching and developing new thinking and innovations, and nurturing other leaders to help them maximize their potential.[153]

MONEY MANAGERS

In addition to looking at women who own wealth, we need to consider the role and impact of women who are managing wealth. There is convincing evidence why asset owners—including pension funds, insurance companies, banks, investment funds, and family offices—will want to put more money into women's hands for management.

Data shows strong comparative performance by women in capital management, mostly attributable to strategic consistency in the face of noise, less overconfidence, and volatility mitigation. Many studies over the last decade or so show comparable results. A July 2019 study by HEC Paris Business School professor Oliver Gottschalg and MVision Private Equity Advisers found that private equity fund managers with gender-diverse investment committees had higher returns compared to their male-only peers.[154] The study found that gender-diverse investment committees outperformed all-male investment committees in alpha (the excess return of an investment relative to its benchmark) by 7%; total value to paid in capital (the ratio of the current value of remaining investments within a fund, plus the total value of all distributions to date, relative to the total amount of capital paid into the fund to date) by 0.52%; and internal rate of return by 12%. The study reviewed the audited performance data on 2,454 investments made by 51 different fund managers across 220 investment vehicles and found that women make up a relatively small portion of executive decision-makers in private equity, occupying just 9.4% of senior positions at private equity firms globally, even though their presence at the table is generally followed by stronger performance.[155] Gottschalg also found that when women were involved in the investment due diligence process in a private equity deal, the underlying portfolio company failure rate was substantially reduced.[156]

Another study by Rothstein Kass showed that women-run hedge funds outperformed the average of larger hedge funds by a margin of six percentage points over six and a half years.[157] The study emphasizes that women investors trade less than men and are able to maintain conviction, even in the face of significant market noise. One study from the Vanguard Group showed that women were 10% less likely to abandon their investments during a market meltdown, choosing to maintain a consistent strategy. Their portfolio-construction strategies often include less trendy, longer-term investments, which may be how they mitigate volatility. This, over time, results in stronger performance.[158]

Growing evidence points to patterns you will not want to ignore. As Meredith Jones declares in her book *Women of the Street: Why Female Money Managers Generate Higher Returns (and How You Can Too)*, "Because you can't escape the impact of behavior on investments, it probably makes sense to at least think about the cognitive and behavioral style of the money managers you hire. . . . Your goal should be to choose money managers who maximize the profitable traits . . . while mitigating your less profitable biases."[159] The female characteristics that we detailed in the section on inherent gender leadership differences—such as not being driven by ego, collaborative and network leadership styles, risk awareness, and having the long view—cannot be ignored as they lead to long-term profitability for companies as well as wealth dividends for individuals.

Case Story: Nia: A Money Manager
Succeeding with Conscious Investing

Women of the World Endowment hosts a monthly Changemakers Series conversation. This series is a highly curated event with twenty to thirty innovators, investors, and actors engaging in an intimate discussion at the intersection of investing, gender, and solving global challenges.

For one of these conversations, Ruth sat down with Kristin Hull, CEO of Nia Impact Capital, to discuss how aligning your investments with your values doesn't mean sacrificing value.[160] Kristin is a conscious investor who works with individuals, families, and organizations to invest in alignment with their values to help create the world they want to see. She launched Nia Global Solutions in 2013 to bring activism and impact investing into the public markets. Its portfolio has outperformed the MSCI ACWI Index since inception. This outperformance is the basis for a challenge that Kristin offers to those investors who don't incorporate social and environmental practices into their portfolios: "We'll see you at the performance chart!"

Ruth: Kristin, how did you get started in the business of conscious investing?

Kristin: I grew up in a trading firm where the mantra was buy low and sell high as often as one possibly could. But I knew that as much as we could harness the financial markets for financial gain, we could make a difference in the world if we invested for social and environmental gains as well.

When I was in charge of our family foundation, we changed the investment policy so that it was the first 100% impact invested foundation in 2007. We weren't in public markets at all, and I hadn't found anything that met my values or that would make the financial returns and the difference that I wanted to make. I looked at every possible public offering and then realized what I was looking for didn't exist. So I set out to build it myself. In the end we launched Nia with the name that means "intention and purpose." What we do all day is try to make the most purpose-driven decisions with every dollar.

Ruth: Can you tell us about some of your best public investments and why you chose them?

Kristin: We certainly like a good deal, so we want to discover underappreciated companies in today's market. When we're evaluating companies, we are "buy and hold" and looking at long-term commitments. We think about this as almost like a private equity play in the public markets because we're looking at companies early. We're getting to know management. That's actually part of our theory of change and our activism. We get in and ask some of the tough questions that we believe will help companies be better. We are considering pipelines of products and services that are addressing our global systemic risks, so everything from health care to sustainable planet to financial inclusion. We're looking for those companies that are working on purpose, and so that makes us pretty different.

Ruth: Can you share a specific example?

Kristin: We made an early investment in Etsy. One of the reasons we love Etsy is that over 80% of the sellers on their platform are women. They are women who really understand business opportunities. One of the things about Etsy is that they do such a good job with creating a positive and inclusive workplace environment that they're able to attract and retain top talent. A lot of the other tech firms struggle with that. Nia helps with best practices, so we have regular conversations with Etsy and the rest of our portfolio companies. Of course, we need to make our clients money, yet we're also here to change the face of finance and of corporate America. Other wins have occurred through shareholder engagement. We vote our proxies in alignment with what we need to see in the world. We're also having strategic conversations about diversity, equity, and inclusion at all our companies.

Ruth: One of the most compelling arguments for a gender-focused, solutions-focused perspective is that it can and usually does mean both better asset performance and better impact performance. Your funds have beaten the MSCI Investable Market Index and the S&P 500 since inception. What's your secret sauce?

Kristin: We're definitely looking to invest at that intersection of environmental sustainability and social justice. We start with our six solution themes using systems thinking and backing up from the concept of just what is needed for people and the planet to not only survive but also to thrive together. We are investing in renewable energies and products we need to solve some of our biggest health-care and inequality issues. We think about what the public markets will reward for and then of course which companies have the best solutions, the best intellectual property, and the ability to build the best teams to execute on the ideas. As you know, past performance is not an indicator of future performance. Having said that, Nia's portfolio has done well outperforming the MSCI ACWI and S&P 500 over the last five years.[161]

We started with a gender focus and have now moved to a strategy supporting full diversity and inclusion in leadership. We're able to use our investor voice to move companies, to get them thinking about diversity, to get them appointing chief diversity officers, to get out their diversity reports. We hope that along the line, they will put practices in place that

FINANCIAL PERFORMANCE AS OF OCTOBER 31, 2021

will help attract and retain diverse talent, which, of course, leads to more and more return on investment.

When it comes to our health-care bucket, we're looking at women and people of color. One topic area that was easy for us to dive into is treatments for sickle cell disease. This primarily affects Black Americans. It gets tricky. When you look at our top five companies working on sickle cell disease, some of them have no people of color in leadership. So how do you balance out the potential of effective treatment for a disease that's really important to a certain community when that community is not represented in the company leadership? We generally devise a strategy before investing about what conversations about issues like these will look like. We like to start when there's at least a hint of a commitment to diversity. We can build off that to push them to improve.

Ruth: Given this excellent performance of your fund, what have been the barriers to attracting other investors to your fund?

Kristin: To get into the financial industry, first they say you need a three-year track record, then they say you need a five-year track record, then you need to have $500 million under management to be considered as a manager. The barriers to creativity in our industry are huge, and for women they're just that much higher. One difference you made, Ruth, was to introduce me to your advisors at some of the big banks. That put Nia on the radar screen at some of the bigger investment houses and has been very helpful. This is how the entire industry changes, one conversation at a time, with the investor voice creating change.

Ruth: How do you think about scaling and growing your business?

Kristin: We need to grow. I don't want us to measure our growth in the traditional way, which is by assets under management. Yet assets under management are our milestones because the more assets we have under management, the more hiring and training we can do. We have a "Change the Face of Finance" internship program. We not only want to attract and train women and people of color into this industry, but we also want to make it really exciting for them.

We are also preparing to launch our mutual fund. This will be a sign that we've been able to democratize this movement and welcome investors with a minimum of one thousand dollars. We are excited about getting this type of a product into 401(k) accounts—which is where most people are investing. We believe that once women and people of color have the option of including a fund like Nia in their retirement accounts, we'll be able to scale and change the way people think about investing. And then of course our voice gets louder with our portfolio corporations—so they'll be that much more likely to take our calls.

BOARDS AND EXECUTIVE TEAMS

Now let us consider in more detail the impact on the bottom line when corporate board directors are women. This area has been studied extensively, and there is enough research that a number of investment strategies have been developed using the data sets. Studies indicate that when women cross the threshold of constituting 30% female of a board's membership, they begin having an impact on the governance of a company. At the 30% level, female board members become more comfortable speaking out and are also more listened to by other board members.[162] Boards with three or more women perform much better in terms of governance metrics, as more of the female traits of risk awareness, collaboration, and long-term thinking become better integrated into their cultures. A study by Adams and Ferreira found that the more gender diverse the board, the more likely a company is to focus on clear communication to employees, prioritize customer satisfaction, consider diversity and corporate social responsibility, and manage downsides better.[163] Data indicates that Fortune 500 firms with female board members did better than those without them when it came to return on equity, return on sales, and return on invested capital as well as a range of other criteria, including share price performance.[164] It's important to note that we are not advocating for all-female boards; rather, gender-balanced boards will be the best-performing ones.

Gender-diverse executive teams also drive stronger financial results. A 2018 McKinsey report cited a statistically significant correlation between greater diversity in leadership teams and financial outperformance. Companies in the top-quartile of gender-diverse executive teams were 21% more likely to see outperformance in profitability as compared to their peers or benchmarks. They were 27% more likely to deliver superior value creation.[165] Credit Suisse released its first research report on this topic in 2014, reviewing 27,000 senior managers at over 3,000 companies covered by Credit Suisse analysts. It dug into whether evidence of robust performance could be linked to gender-diverse senior teams. The study has been repeated for a number of years. For the period 2013–2016, the data verified the link to superior share performance. The research found that "[Companies] where women accounted for 25 percent of senior leadership outperformed at a compound annual growth rate of 2.8 percent; this increased to 4.7 percent at companies where women comprised 33 percent of senior leadership; and then jumped to 10.3 percent at companies where more than 50 percent of senior leaders are women compared with a 1 percent annual decline for MSCI ACWI index over the same period."[166]

These results could be attributed to what Anita Woolley and colleagues described in a 2010 report as "the collective intelligence of a group and how it is linked to the style and type of interaction between the group members." Specifically, Woolley and her fellow researchers demonstrated that collective group intelligence was higher when (a) the social sensitivity of the individual group members was higher, (b) there was a more even distribution in the conversation between individual group members (rather than having the conversation dominated by one or two people), and (c) there were more women in the group.[167]

Research is now evaluating which senior leadership roles improve corporate performance. In 2019, *Bloomberg* published an article on how female CFOs can make a difference, finding that they generate increased profits and higher share prices in their first two years in the role.[168] The same study shows that on average, there is a 6% increase in profits and an 8% bump in stock performance compared to overall performance under male predecessors, including the male's first two years.[169] A study by S&P Global Market Intelligence, based on a review of companies in the Russell 3000 over a seventeen-year period, indicated $1.8 trillion of additional cumulative profits for companies with female CFOs.[170] The researchers attribute the better performance to "survivorship bias," meaning that because male CFOs outnumber female CFOs (6.5 to 1), the women who make it into the positions are on average really good at their jobs.[171]

This evidence is leading such respected capital markets entities as the Nasdaq to signal that male-only boards are no longer acceptable. Less than 75% of Nasdaq companies have at least one woman and one underrepresented minority or LGBT+ member on the board.[172] In December 2020, Nasdaq announced that it had filed a proposal with the US Securities and Exchange Commission to adopt new diversity listing rules. The proposal was approved by the commission in August 2021, and the new listing rules require companies listed on Nasdaq's US exchange to publicly disclose diversity statistics regarding their board of directors. Additionally, the rules require most Nasdaq-listed companies to have or provide reasons they do not have at least two diverse directors, including one who self-identifies as female, and another as either an underrepresented minority or LGBTQ+.[173]

Other examples of capital market entities initiating policies requiring diverse boards can be found in the United Kingdom, where considerable progress has been made in board diversity. The representation of women on boards of the Financial Times Stock Exchange (FTSE) 100 companies stood at 32.4% in 2019 compared to 12.5% in 2011. The companies in both the FTSE 100 and FTSE 250 achieved on average 33% female board membership by the end of 2020. The latest requirement by the UK regulator is for companies to have at least one minority board member by 2024.[174] Other countries are stepping up and enacting legislation to address this issue as well.

There are several ways to encourage companies to increase the number of women on their boards. One is to set quotas for all companies registered within a country. These quotas can have penalties attached to them, but many do not. For example, the 2010 Kenyan constitution established a precedent that elected bodies should have no more than two-thirds of their members be of the same gender.[175] This is extended to corporate boards through the Guidelines on Corporate Governance Practices list included in the Capital Markets Act of 2012.[176] These quotas and encouragements do not have penalties attached, so companies are still largely in control of their own voluntary gender-diversity measures. As of 2019, women make up 24% of nonexecutive directors on boards in Kenya, which still falls below the 33% minimum encouraged by the quotas but is higher than the 12% of female makeup of boards that existed in 2012.[177]

Norway, however, instituted a binding requirement in 2008 that the boards of all publicly traded companies consist of at least 40% women.[178] This requirement had mixed results. While the percentage of women on boards did go up, the percentage of women in the overall population holding director positions did not change. This created a phenomenon known as "golden skirts," in which the number of women directors remained static while each of the women sat on more boards.[179] Another unforeseen consequence of this legislation was that a number of companies delisted from the stock exchange, going private or relisting on exchanges in countries that did not require gender diversity. Delisting was particularly prevalent among companies that had a smaller share of women on their boards prior to the quota. Of course, our research indicates that those companies that chose to delist rather than diversify were being shortsighted, as the evidence shows that gender diversity on corporate boards leads to markedly improved company performance.[180] Because these companies no longer share information publicly, we cannot know for sure how they fared after delisting.

FOUNDERS AND ENTREPRENEURS

The data is clear. Start-up companies with diverse talent and women on leadership teams outperform their less-diverse peers across a number of dimensions, including innovation, risk management, and long-term asset management. Studies show that over the past ten years, new businesses with at least one female founder outperformed their all-male counterparts.[181] One study showed that the outperformance is significant: over a ten-year period, companies with a female founder performed 63% better than those with all-male founding teams.[182] In addition, start-up teams with women founders generate more than double the revenue per dollar invested than those with all-male founders—78 cents versus 31 cents.[183]

This data seems hard to believe because we do not hear of many female-founded unicorns (start-up companies that end up with valuations greater than one billion dollars). Our sense is that because female-founded/led companies receive less capital investment, each dollar must do more. Hence, each dollar is spent with extensive consideration for risk mitigation. Capital efficiency is good but after a certain point it can lead to decelerating growth. Given the strong performance data, we have wondered what would happen if more of the money invested in venture capital ($300.5 billion in 2020) and private equity ($3.2 trillion in 2020) were invested in teams that are gender diverse.[184] The return to investors would be significant, as start-up companies are often valued on multiples of their current revenues. Today most venture capital investors back founding teams that most closely reflect the investment team's demographic identity: gender, race, alma mater, or regions they reside in. This may explain why most venture capitalists average one successful investment (defined as an investment with more than $1 billion in valuation or a company whose successful exit repays investors and generates profits) for every ten investments made.[185]

Other metrics, such as job creation and innovation, support the argument for investing more capital in women-owned businesses. According to the US Census Bureau, from 2007 to 2015, women-owned businesses created 1.24 million more jobs compared to male-owned firms, largely due to the increased number of women-owned businesses.[186] Greater investment would allow these businesses to scale faster rather than rely on organic growth. More money would enable recruitment and retention of talent as well as greater spending on research and development that would lead to better innovations. This is important; a report by the Institute for Women's Policy Research covered in the *Atlantic* showed that technological innovations patented by gender-diverse teams seem to fare better over the long term. According to this report, information technology patents that list gender-diverse teams are cited with disproportionate frequency in subsequent patent applications, "suggesting that greater diversity may lead to the development of patents that are more useful and successful."[187] The same report indicated that four decades ago, 3% of all patents listed at least one woman inventor. As of 2010, this number had increased to nearly 19%, a substantial increase, but this means that 81% of patents still included no women.[188] Recall from the previous section the story of the female scientists who were major players in the development of the COVID-19 vaccines. More funding for women scientists like Drs. Karikó and Corbett can lead to greater positive impacts for our collective health and wealth.

In the United States, which has the most robust landscape for early-stage company investing, we see dismal numbers for investments in female founders and female-owned companies. About 3% of venture capital goes to women-owned start-ups, and an even smaller percentage of private equity capital into growth companies goes to women-owned companies. On average, women entrepreneurs get smaller loans across every debt product and often pay higher interest rates, despite their better repayment record.[189] This is astounding given that more than 36% of all businesses in the United States are owned by women.[190] These businesses continue despite a lack of capital investment, showing the resilience of these business owners—and missed opportunities. What would US growth look like if these businesses received the capital support they need to grow? How would this impact multiply across the world, where women entrepreneurs are in abundance? If companies with female founders and gender-diverse teams could access capital equally from start-up to growth stages, the economic pie would grow significantly.

This disparity in capital access is particularly relevant in the age of COVID-19. The data from 2020 is still emerging, but as women-owned businesses tend to have less capital runway, smaller working-capital facilities from their banks, and limited equity capital to support operations, it is likely that a disproportionate number of female-owned small businesses shut down due to COVID-19 restrictions. Given all we know about the potential of these companies, this hit to the stability of our communities and the growth of the economy is unacceptable.

DEBTHOLDERS

Across all types of debt, female borrowers exhibit the same sensibilities and behaviors regarding financial decision-making as we see in female fund managers, CEOs, board directors, and entrepreneurs. In general, women tend to be more aware of the risks that come with accepting debt, are more likely to use loans to create revenue (rather than to speculate), and are more dependable repaying loans.

Let's first look at small business loans. From 2017 to 2019, the IFC investigated the business case for providing debt to women-owned small- and medium-sized enterprises (SMEs) in the developing world. They found that for all three years, women-owned SMEs had significantly lower than average nonperforming loan (NPL) ratios. Between 2015 and 2018, they found that female portfolios had NPL ratios of 3.6, 4.0, 3.7, and 3.0%, while the male portfolios had ratios of 4.3, 4.8, 4.7, and 4.9%.[191] These numbers have a marked negative impact on the profitability of financial institutions. At most banks, exposure to male clients is greater and the losses in those portfolios are higher, leading to lower returns for investors.

Another important IFC study looked at SMEs in Vietnam. This study used both quantitative and qualitative research methods to evaluate the demand and supply for SME loans in that country. They surveyed 322 women-owned businesses and 178 men-owned businesses. They reached several relevant conclusions. First, they described the women's approach to risk as being different from men's because of "their focus on long-term goals and greater awareness of risk. In other words, they tend to measure and analyze risk more meticulously, rather than simply following their intuition."[192] Second, banks reported lower nonperforming loans among women entrepreneurs (one bank reporting NPLs of 0.95% for women-owned SMEs versus 2.17% for men-owned SMEs).[193]

In September 2019, *Financial Express* also reported that in India, women-led SMEs are more reliable in repaying loans than SMEs led by men.[194] One theory is that women are better at saving money so they tend to use loans for revenue-generating purposes rather than discretionary spending. Both factors would contribute to women-run small businesses using debt more effectively to produce a profit and to better position themselves to repay their loans. The article also suggested that "women are psychologically more intended to make an investment decision in collaboration with the companies that address social equality, environmental sustainability, and gender diversity. Hence, they remain self-motivated to build a stronger relationship with such companies by repaying the loan amount timely [*sic*]."[195]

In the United States, a 2016 Urban Institute study showed that single women were better at paying their mortgages than single men.[196] Ironically, despite this more-reliable repayment pattern, the study also shows that women were given less favorable interest rates and were more often denied mortgages than men. Holding all credit risk factors constant, the study's authors concluded that women did a much better job of repayment than their credit scores would suggest.[197] A recent study by Experian that compared credit scores and debt repayment between men and women found that women on average have a higher credit score (675 versus 670 for men) and an 8.1% lower incidence of late mortgage payments.[198] This analysis also revealed that women tend to have more debt and more open credit cards. But even in the face of that higher debt burden, they were more likely to repay their debts on time.[199]

An interesting study conducted in Chile by the Inter-American Development Bank determined that women were nearly 15% less likely to be approved for loans than men—even though women have higher repayment rates than men in that country.[200] The study concluded that this deficit in lending to women was due to pro-male biases in the lending officers. They estimated that "9.9 percent of expected bank profits are not capitalized due to taste-based discrimination (equivalent to annual foregone profits of US$13,400 per case), an inefficiency cost equal to the annual wage bill of 1,500 loan officers or 18 percent of all loan officers working in the Chilean banking system."[201]

Microfinance is the model of microcredit started by Nobel Prize–winning Bangladeshi social entrepreneur Muhammad Yunus. In a microfinance system, small personal or business loans are given to individuals who otherwise would not be able to qualify for commercial loans. These programs have been successful lifting people and communities out of poverty and have proliferated around the world. There is much research on women as debtholders that uses data on microfinance. Women make up about 80% of microfinance clients, but we hesitate to discuss microfinance in this book because too often the financial services industry has associated women with microcredit only.[202] It is essential that we dismantle the "women = microcredit" mental model and build the "women = all forms of capital" mental model. That being said, there is extensive evidence from the microfinance sector that shows the strong performance of women as debtholders. Women who receive microloans repay them reliably and quickly.[203] In addition, studies from multiple countries demonstrate that when women have cash and some control over household spending, the money they have is more likely to go toward products and services that are valuable for the whole family (such as appliances or children's education) when compared with men. Women share their money with the whole family more fairly.[204] This means that a lender will get two types of rewards if they microlend to women—more reliable return on their investment and more stability in the communities they are lending to.

Whether we are looking at microfinance models in ultra-poor global communities, lending programs for small businesses, or mortgages for the US middle class, the evidence shows us that women are more reliable debtors. They are more likely to pay back their loans and more likely to use the money they borrow to create greater stability in their communities and improve the lives of those around them. If women are consistently more reliable borrowers, why are banks and other lenders not rewarding them with better interest rates? Why do they make it harder for them to secure loans?

There is one global investment organization that rewards women's debt repayment behavior. As part of an effort to boost its recruitment of female investment managers, the Swedish global investment organization EQT recently pledged to pay its lenders a higher interest rate if EQT failed to recruit more women to its investment team.[205] EQT was using this commitment as an incentive to drive their own recruitment of female investment managers. We expect to see other lenders demand that corporate borrowers include women as financial decision makers, or at least offer incentives for them to do so.

LANDOWNERS

We've presented evidence for how women's participation in financial decision-making across many types of capital results in improved financial returns. Do we also see improved financial returns when women are investors in land? The answer, once again, is yes. When women own land, they use it for the financial benefit of themselves, their families, their communities, and their investors—in the instances where they have investors.

When we look at gender analyses of control of public companies, investment funds, venture capital, or early stage companies, we are usually talking about well-educated women. Although these women have less access to capital than their male peers, they are still relatively well-off and well-resourced. When we talk about land ownership, most existing data on the difference between financial returns based on landowner gender comes from agriculture and small subsistence farmers. In less-developed countries, these are often women who have fewer resources and sit at the bottom of the socioeconomic pyramid.

In many countries women are still prohibited from owning or inheriting land, and less than 20% of agricultural land in developing countries is owned by women.[206] Women often are not in a position of control of the resources—the land, training, fertilizers, equipment, and so on. And they are rarely in positions to control large industrial farming operations in developing or industrialized countries. Yet women make up more than 60% of the rural labor force and are responsible for up to 80% of African food production.[207] In the United States, women are taking on a greater role in agriculture as well, owning or co-owning up to 43% of US farmland—nearly 388 million acres. This number has increased because men who work in agriculture are retiring and their roles are being taken up by women.[208]

Agriculture is another example of a sector where women are closest to the problems that need to be solved. Women make up well over half of the agricultural workforce around the world and are much more likely to be working the land while the male heads of households make financial decisions about the properties and negotiate with big agriculture companies or governments for resources.[209] And it is often the men who receive and control the capital necessary to succeed in an industry that is reliant on financing. African women farmers receive less than 10% of the credit provided to farmers across the continent.[210] In a survey of 95 countries, women in agriculture, forestry, and fishery receive only 10% of the aid allocated to those industries and only 5% of all agricultural extension services.[211] In most of the countries surveyed, women-headed households had 5–10% less access to credit than households headed by men—credit that is crucial to make capital investments and buy essential inputs.[212]

When women have the resources to make a small farm successful, they can turn a profit and use land more productively than men. We see that there is a "trickle-up effect" when women subsistence farmers own their own land. They tend to invest in their families (for instance, by allocating more resources to enable their children to attend school) and their communities (employing their friends and neighbors), creating a localized profit that benefits their communities more broadly. This in turn creates economic stability both at the local and national levels.[213]

In 2014, Root Capital conducted a thorough investigation of the intersection of gender and agriculture around the world.[214] They noted an inherently inequitable system in terms of women's decision-making power and access to resources. An analysis in 2012 from the United Nations Food and Agriculture Organization (FAO) determined that "if women had the same access to productive resources as men, they could increase their yields on their farms by 20–30%."[215] In another report, FAO calculated that if women had the same access to resources as men, it "would raise total agricultural output in developing countries by 2.5–4%, in turn reducing the number of hungry people in the world by 12–17%."[216]

Investing in rural women significantly increases farm productivity and improves rural livelihoods for everyone, not only for women. The Root Capital report identified women as influencers throughout the agricultural value chain, whether working as landowners, accountants, commercial vendors, field officers, or field workers.[217] Root Capital's research showed that "when women are in any of these roles, they provide a different value to women and families in the same positions."[218] This value includes an increase in farming training programs for women and improvements in farm productivity. And when this increase in productivity results in increased income for local women, this Root Capital research once again detailed the trickle-up effect where women spend money on their families for food, school fees, and health-care costs, thereby contributing to the overall stability of both the households and the communities.

In addition to increasing social stability—an important risk-reduction factor for emerging markets investors—the differences in how men and women reinvest in their families, farms, and communities have long-range economic impacts on global surpluses. A 2021 literature review published by *Journal of Development Studies* looked at dozens of studies regarding women farmers in the developing world and found that women farmers' reinvestment differs in three key ways. Women grow more diverse and nutritious crops, which result in increased household dietary diversity and nutrition through subsistence farming and business income from agricultural products. Women also intercrop more frequently, a practice of cultivating more than one crop in the same field. This practice preserves soil quality and lowers soil erosion, thereby increasing long-term productivity. And because women typically use their earnings to increase household spending on food and education, resulting in better nutrition and educational outcomes for their children, this leads to higher labor productivity and lower health costs further down the line.[219]

These different reinvestment practices could significantly decrease the cost of treating malnutrition incurred by the health-care systems of low-income countries, a cost that usually consumes between 1% and 11% of countries' total public health budgets.[220] The World Bank estimated in 2006 that economic loss due to malnutrition could be 2–3% of a nation's GDP, and that the productivity lost due to malnutrition could amount to more than 10% of a person's lifetime earnings.[221] When women control a greater share of agricultural capital, it will mitigate economic drag as well.

More sustainable crop and soil management also has direct economic benefits. Prioritizing sustainable land management would reduce the annual loss of US$300 billion sustained by farmers and consumers across the globe due to land degradation. Meanwhile, every dollar put toward combating land degradation yields a return of US$5 on average.[222]

Since we know women reinvest in their communities at a higher rate than men do, and since women make up such a huge and growing part of the agricultural sector, investing in and securing women's right to own land could cause a positive ripple effect across global markets. When we empower women in positions of agricultural leadership, we get two benefits: we create large-scale economic growth and strengthen global sustainability efforts and community infrastructure, both of which lead to better conditions for investment into emerging markets and better overall financial performance. This phenomenon is significant enough that we recommend that folks who are interested in investing in emerging markets should evaluate women's access to land ownership. Consider any existing laws that prohibit women's land ownership as a strong deterrent to investing in these markets.

Land organization is central to sustaining healthy communities and healthy individuals. It has an impact on every facet of human life, from economic productivity to environmental sustainability to public safety to physical and mental health. Women are stewards of the land—and of the communities that live on it—and have found innovative ways to support the people and the environments around them, rural or urban, in ways that generate significant economic uplift.

Though women have historically been excluded from fields like real estate development, occupying just 4% of major investment positions at real estate development companies in 2011, many have now become leaders in urban planning areas ranging from sustainable design and accessibility to economic development and mitigating urban precarity.[223] If women landowners have the opportunity to increase their power and influence, we could reap massive economic benefits and have stronger, healthier communities.

MORE THAN FINANCIAL PERFORMANCE

In addition to posting strong financial performance, women are more likely to be environmentally and socially conscious investors. A report by the Business and Sustainable Development Commission indicated that female financial advisors were 42% more interested in recommending investments with social and environmental benefits and more likely to perceive global issues—such as pollution, conflict, and inequality—as "very serious" considerations.[224] The report also found them to be more concerned about environmental problems and to be "sustainably minded consumers."[225] These concerns led some women to begin focusing on environmental, social, and governance (ESG) investing.

ESG (also described as "values-based," "socially responsible," or "sustainable") investing is that which takes into consideration the environmental, social, and governance impacts of the companies in portfolios. The practice dates to the 1800s when the Methodist church encouraged its members to restrict their investments in companies that traded in alcohol, tobacco, weapons, or gambling.[226] In the 1960s, the practice became more popular, especially as a tool for global political action.

Over the past twenty years, ESG investing has become more extensive, evolving to include strategies for values investing across all asset classes including public equities, fixed income, private equity, venture capital, and real estate. This more recent wave started in Europe where governments developed standards and guidelines in the early 2000s.[227] In those days, women investors and financial advisors were more likely to be leading most investment firms' ESG programs, which were then treated as niche offerings for philanthropic or values-based investors. Little attention was paid by the mainstream financial markets and the bigger banks, largely because it was assumed that there would be decreased financial returns when compared to traditional financial products that don't take ESG performance into consideration. This expectation that investors would make less money resulted in little demand for ESG-aligned financial products. As the trend has become more popular around the world, it has become clear that not only can ESG investing produce significant positive changes in environment and social outcomes and the governance of companies but, also result in significant financial returns.

As ESG has become an accepted investment strategy, benchmarks have developed to evaluate performance and guide investment strategies. The case study that follows shows how one key benchmark emerged.

Case Story: Equileap:
Indexing Inclusion for Investment Returns

When I (Ruth) began my new career as a philanthropist and impact investor in 2014, I was looking for a measurement approach that would help identify public companies that are good for women. If the investments of the Tara Health Foundation were to be 100% aligned with the overall mission of the organization, there needed to be an evidence-based rationale for the public companies and mutual funds added to the portfolio. At that time, many investors were interested in screening public equities for gender benefits, and the state of the art was to include companies that had women on their boards of directors or the senior leadership teams. These were the only data points readily available to the public. However, my take was that while having women in these most-senior positions within companies was certainly a good thing, it was an inadequate measure of the company's overall benefits to their workers or the communities in which they operated. Using grant dollars from the Tara Health Foundation, I commissioned the team at the Wharton Social Impact Initiative (WSII) to establish an evidence-based framework for measuring a company's impact on the women they employ. In November 2018, WSII published the Four for Women report. The framework identified representation, pay, health, and job satisfaction as the measures that mattered most for women.[228] Using this Four for Women framework as a baseline, I reviewed the existing corporate measurement vendors in the field and was excited to find that an organization called Equileap was already using a robust scorecard that mirrored the measures outlined in Four for Women.

Equileap is a social enterprise that collects data across 19 criteria from roughly 4,000 publicly listed companies across the world, covering everything from the gender pay gap and shared parental leave policies to flexible working arrangements and diversity in the supply chain.[229] The aim is to help investors make better-informed decisions about which companies they believe will make sustainable returns. Indices using Equileap's data are tracked by financial products with millions of dollars successfully invested. For example, as detailed in the graph on page 110, from 2011 to 2021 the Equileap Global Gender Equality 100 Leaders Net TR Index, which is based on the Equileap scorecard, had an annualized outperformance of 2% against the MSCI World EW Net Index.[230] The UBS Global Gender Equality Exchange-Traded Fund (ETF) (ticker: GENDER) tracks this Equileap index, and by December 2021 it reached US$904 million in assets under management (AUM).[231] As investors catch on to the power of gender equity to fuel successful companies and successful investment products, they turn to data providers such as Equileap to create the indices embedded in the ETFs. At the end of 2021, there were several billion dollars in AUM in publicly listed products based on the Equileap scorecard as well as dozens of leading financial institutions globally using it for screening and investment purposes on a daily basis.

Gender equality is not just about the number of men and women on the board or in senior management, which is why Equileap collects metrics from all levels of the workforce. True equality in the workplace takes comprehensive, concentrated, and consistent effort, and it benefits all genders. Since Equileap launched in 2016, there has been steady progress in how companies perform on the Equileap scorecard. The number one company globally has seen its gender equality score improve over the years to reach 74% in 2021.[232] The collateral benefit of this strategy is that investors get better-performing products, workers have more equitable workplaces, and companies are more sustainable.

Equileap Global Top 100 Equal Weighted Index / MSCI World EW Index - Daily Performance 2011–2021

— Solative Equileap Global Gender Equality 100 Leaders Net TR Index   —— MSCI World Equal Weighted Net Index

THE BOTTOM LINE

In this chapter, we have outlined the evidence that having female financial decision-makers investing in all asset classes lead to stronger financial returns. In the next chapter, we will turn our attention to outlining the reasons why having females in decision-making positions is essential given the current state of the world. After that, we will look at the financial risks to your portfolio performance that come from not embracing inclusivity.

CHAPTER 3
WINNING IN THE NEXT ECONOMY

THE XX EDGE

WE ARE ON THE THRESHOLD OF BOTH AN ECONOMIC dislocation and disruption—what we are calling the "next economy." If we view dislocations as forces from the natural world that disturb the usual state of things, such as the impact of climate change or pandemics, and disruptions as human-caused change in industries and markets, from new technologies or increased social inequality, then we can say that the world is going through both dislocation and disruption. And maybe that is what is different about this moment.

How our economies emerge and who rebuilds them matter. Given the scale of the challenges and the scope of opportunity, the global economy needs to rebuild for growth. If there is more wealth created through commerce, employment, and productivity, then the whole economic pie grows, creating more benefits for everyone to share. Individuals or communities don't need to fight over small pieces if the overall pie is bigger. We can make a bigger pie by leveraging all human talent. If you partner with female decision-makers and utilize a gender analysis in your investment decisions, you can take advantage of the next economy, better your returns, and lower your risk.

A DISLOCATED AND DISRUPTED WORLD

Many of the current social movements around the world are fundamentally based on the assumption that the pie is shrinking. Many wealthy individuals go along with this argument, which is ironic given that their personal pie is growing faster than at any other time in history, including the last expansion after the subprime financial crisis.[233] Take Peter Thiel, who said in 2012, "In a world without technological progress you have a zero-sum society in which there has to be a loser for every winner. It is not clear that capitalism would work in that sort of society, I certainly don't think democratic government could work—it works by having a growing pie in which you forge compromises in which you divvy up the pie. When the pie stops growing, politics gets polarized, and people get really angry with each other even when there are no differences between them."[234]

Thiel is correct about the need for a growing pie for our institutions to function. What is missing from his view is the fact that we can grow the pie by including more talent in innovation and capital allocation. Sadly, so many people don't see the possibility of making things better for all by better leveraging all talent. From the fight against better wages, to the emergence of populist movements across the world, to the scramble for geographic and ethnic domination, we see evidence of people buying into the notion of a zero-sum game. Although some resources are constrained, the supply of human talent is not. Throughout recent history, significant global dislocations and disruptions— like the one we are going through—have been followed by periods of sustained expansion, not contraction.

We are in a moment of dislocation, characterized by record-breaking climate-related headwinds, with unprecedented numbers of climate disasters in rapid succession and of people displaced due to climate change. According to the UN's "Human Cost of Disasters" report, from 2000 to 2019 climate disasters have affected over 4 billion lives and are responsible for the deaths of at least 1.23 million people.[235]

We are also in a moment of disruption. McKinsey Global Institute's "The Four Global Forces Breaking All the Trends" identifies the elements of disruption as (1) geographic shifts related to industrial and urban transformations across regions and within countries, (2) the acceleration of the technology revolution, (3) the world's changing demographics, and (4) extensive global trade and human connections.[236] Given all these trends, how can we be optimistic that the world is set for a period of economic expansion?

The answer is that we see the potential that will come from using the talent and knowledge of everyone in the world. This will lead to innovation, risk mitigation, and building a better global economy. This requires moving away from the traditional paradigm—which assumes that men with money in wealthy nations can build solutions to every problem and that everyone else, everywhere else, will accept the outcomes—toward a total talent paradigm in which those who have historically been excluded from the decision-making are actively providing innovation and solutions. A paradigm that engages all talent, especially people from those populations most impacted by dislocation and disruption, is essential to improving our individual and collective health and wealth.

To win in the next economy, investors need to recognize the world's current challenges, acknowledge the acceleration of change, and embrace the potential for more solution-building, fueled by more-inclusive talent pools and capital markets. The evolution of global economic growth toward more service-related jobs favors a more inclusive talent paradigm. Data from the World Bank shows a steady decline in agricultural and industrial jobs and a marked increase in service employment as automation takes over tasks previously performed by human labor.[237] In the United States, this shift to a service economy has been driven by a combination of automation, offshoring, and recession-related plant closures. Manufacturing jobs have fallen from 18 million in 1990 to approximately 12.5 million in 2021.[238] The United States has gone from having 36 states with manufacturing-dominant economies to only seven, with retail and health care being the largest employers across all states.[239] About 57% of retail industry employees are women.[240] Over 60% of health-care employees in the United States are women.[241]

Beyond the United States, the share of global employment accounted for by the service industry has increased significantly in the past three decades, from 34.43% in 1991 to 50% in 2019.[242] In addition to these shifts in global markets, some countries, such as Sri Lanka and India, appear to have largely skipped over manufacturing as their central industry entirely and have developed directly into service economies.[243]

Service and retail jobs have been dominated by female talent, so women are already well prepared to step into leadership roles in many service-oriented sectors. Unfortunately, it hasn't happened yet. In 2019, twenty-nine S&P 500 companies were retail companies, but only ten of those companies were led by women.[244] Ideally, if over half of retail employees are women, shouldn't more than one-third of the sector's CEOs be women as well?[245] Similarly, women make up over 60% of entry-level health-care jobs but only 30% of C-suite and vice-presidential jobs in the health-care system. If women hold well over half of the entry-level jobs in health care, we should see more women in decision-making positions in these sectors too.[246]

On average, the American health-care industry is more female than any other sector of corporate America except for media and entertainment. McKinsey's research also found that there is no promotional gap between women and men for the first few rungs of the health-care professional ladder. In fact, approximately 102 women are promoted in health care for every 100 men. This higher rate of promotion holds true until the management level, where there is a drop in the percentage of women who serve in upper management and leadership positions.[247] According to McKinsey, this is likely due to "structural challenges (such as hiring and advancement practices), institutional barriers allowing underlying biases to persist, and impact of the daily work environment not promoting an inclusive and supportive experience for all employees."[248] In other words, despite the health-care industry doing well with female promotions at the lower levels, it perpetuates barriers that prevent women from becoming leaders, as is also observed in other industries.

OPPORTUNITIES FOR ACCELERATION, INNOVATION, AND INCLUSIVITY

Climate

One of the main impacts of climate change on people has been displacement. The World Bank estimates that by 2050, Latin America, sub-Saharan Africa, and Southeast Asia will generate 143 million more climate migrants due to desertification, sea-level rise, air pollution, and shifting rain patterns.[249] For example, 2017 saw the largest documented number of displaced people in human history, about 68.5 million, with at least one-third of them being displaced due to climate-related reasons.[250] One unfortunate consequence of climate migration will be that talented individuals will try to move to areas where their skills will be included and rewarded, leaving some regions short on human capital to address challenges there. This means that the areas that don't prioritize diversity will then experience a depletion of their workforce talent, including the talent that could help with mitigating climate crises. What we need is a universal prioritization of utilizing inclusive talent to prevent this harm. Investors can play a role, investing in talent "where it is" to create incentives for people to stay and thrive in place.

If human displacement is not enough to make you concerned, consider the rising cost of climate disasters across the world. Larry Fink, the CEO of BlackRock, the world's largest asset manager, recognizes the cost to investors. In his 2021 CEO letter he wrote, "In the past year, people have seen the mounting physical toll of climate change in fires, droughts, flooding and hurricanes. They have begun to see the direct financial impact as energy companies take billions in climate-related write-downs on stranded assets and regulators focus on climate risk in the global financial system. They are also increasingly focused on the significant economic opportunity that the transition will create, as well as how to execute it in a just and fair manner. No issue ranks higher than climate change on our clients' lists of priorities. They ask us about it nearly every day."[251] The National Oceanic and Atmospheric Administration only started recording billion-dollar climate events in 1980, but 40% of these events have occurred in the last decade, with 2017 being the most expensive year on record, at $334 billion, and 2020 experiencing the highest number of billion-dollar events on record, at 22 events.[252] Even the richest country in the world cannot afford to keep paying for unmitigated climate change. Right now, only a small percentage of people are engaging with the climate challenge. That's not enough. Costs will accrue at even faster rates if we do not have changes.

In January 2021, Texas experienced some of the lowest temperatures it had seen in forty years.[253] Known for its heat in the summer and warm temperatures even in the winter months, the state instead experienced freezing temperatures and ice caused by a polar vortex—a phenomenon caused by warming air over the Arctic pushing frigid air south. Although freezing temperatures are not unheard of in Texas, they have been rare. With the increased frequency of polar vortexes due to climate change, Texans are looking at the possibility of extreme freezes every other year or even annually.[254] The unprecedented demand for heat overloaded the electric grid and triggered blackouts, leaving thousands cut off from power, potable water, and sewage management. The impact was far-reaching, including cutting off at-home access to medical equipment such as oxygen tanks that patients need to survive. At least 151 people died from the catastrophic storm and blackout, and data suggests that number could be even five times higher.[255]

These trends show up around the world, where climate-related disasters have increased by 83% from 3,656 disasters in the two decades between 1980 and 1999 to 6,681 disasters in the 2000–2019 era.[256] The cost of rebuilding homes and lives harms household wealth. These disasters also impact health, affecting over 4 billion lives and causing at least 1.23 million deaths globally.[257] A comprehensive use of human talent to reduce greenhouse gas emissions and develop alternative energy technology and systems could help stem this vicious tide and will mitigate downside risk. This will save companies money, grow economies, and create jobs.

Including women in building solutions can reduce the impact of climate change on human societies. Women are already critical actors in climate change mitigation. Data shows us that women are more likely to be environmentally conscious investors and consumers, which make them critical actors in demand-side climate mitigation. Women are working to improve access to critical resources—for example, women borrowers receive 87% of water and sanitation microloans.[258] In India, local government councils with women's representation have spearheaded the implementation of 62% more drinking water projects than in areas with councils without female representation.[259]

Climate challenges are exacerbating food insecurity around the world, and as investors it will be essential to screen opportunities that include women if we want to solve this crisis. If the same resources that are provided for male farmers were given to female farmers, the total agricultural output of developing countries would be boosted by 2.5 to 4%, and the number of undernourished people in the world would drop by 100 to 150 million (12 to 17%).[260] When able to fully participate in the economy, women contribute to both the financial and social stability of their families, communities, and countries. With more stable economies, greater investments could help prepare, protect, and support populations against climate disasters. By investing in women, we can diminish food shortages and make more money.

Climate change mitigation efforts present a large investment potential. The IMF recognized in a June 2021 report that a significant amount of investment required to stabilize the climate will have to come from the private sector.[261] One can look at losses related to weather and climate change as a measure of the potential investment opportunity, with the payoff from these investments being the reduction or elimination of these losses. Given that $100.2 billion was lost in 2020, the dollar potential is big.[262]

Climate change affects the insurance industry. Even if we slow the rate of change, insurance companies are still projected to spend $52 billion by 2050 on claims from the damage to coastal cities.[263] If we do nothing about the rising temperatures, then insurers will spend $1 trillion on coastal cities by 2050—if they still will be writing policies covering these areas. The opportunity grows if we include inland areas that are susceptible to forest fires, polar vortexes, and landslides.[264] The insurance industry recognizes the potential to stem these losses, investing $23 billion in emissions reductions and related technologies as of 2012.[265]

About 2.6 billion people today use solid fossil fuels such as coal, wood, crop waste, or dung as their primary source of energy at home.[266] Cookstoves represent more than 25% of global black carbon emissions.[267] Further, the World Health Organization (WHO) estimates that exposure to smoke from cooking is the fifth-worst risk factor for disease in developing countries and causes almost two million premature deaths per year—more than malaria or tuberculosis.[268] In addition, women and girls in some regions that primarily use polluting fuels spend an average of 18 hours per week collecting fuel for their families. This chore increases their vulnerability to personal attack and takes time away from more productive activities such as attending school.[269]

Savvy investors see the overlap between investing in women and investments in climate change mitigation. In the developing world, broadening access to clean cook-stoves and solar lanterns (the acquisition of which is driven by women) represents one of the smartest opportunities to make money and reduce the air pollution that results from climate change.

Statistics from the US automotive industry back up the idea of women being climate-friendly consumers. Even a decade ago, an analysis of new vehicle registrations conducted by automotive data company R. L. Polk showed that women gravitated toward smaller, more fuel-efficient cars more often than men.[270] Investing in sustainable energy products is an effective way to improve the environment and seize the expansive female consumer market.

As climate change affects food security, it will drive up food prices. The World Bank estimates that the spike in global food prices since 2008 has pushed 44 million people into poverty in environments where food is scarce.[271] This has heightened the need for an inclusive agenda when looking at how the world will feed its population, and women hold the key. As investors, we can increase our returns by selecting programs that seek to improve food security that target women who currently have less access to inputs, credit, value chains and markets, and technical advancements related to improving their harvests.

As previously indicated, women make up an estimated 50% of all small-scale farmers globally and play a significant role in the production of subsistence food. But the investment gap in women farmers is huge. For example, women receive less than 10% of credit allocated to small-scale farmers in Africa.[272] Those women farmers who do receive loans receive less than they need. This perpetuates an imbalance in capital access, especially in jurisdictions where financial institutions are asset-based lenders; as land ownership is weighted toward men, men access capital more easily. The UN Food and Agriculture Organization estimates that food production would rise by 20 to 30% if women had access to the same production resources as men.[273]

Women disproportionately care about and manage the food consumption needs of their families and their communities.[274] Their food-spending choices are for adequate and nutritious food for their families, but they also care about the protection of the environment for current and future generations. Investors can go further and influence the consumption choices of communities through women, who often make the household purchasing decisions for their families. Corporations can develop products from climate-safe processes that also meet the need for women to feed healthier families. French food giant Danone's 2016 climate policy report stated, "Danone's mission is to bring health through food to the largest number of people across the world. We believe that food is health's most significant partner and recognize that everything we eat depends on the earth that it grows in or feeds on. As gardeners of this planet, we have a duty to responsibly and sustainably manage its resources. New ways can and will be found to better serve this generation and the next, and to bring healthy, affordable food and safe water to the greatest number of people."[275] On the other end of the corporate spectrum is woman-owned Miyoko's Creamery, whose vegan products are sold in US grocery stores. Miyoko has a "compassion-centric mission (from-farmer-to-table) to create the blueprint for the animal-free dairy food system of tomorrow, for the urgent salvation of our planet and all that we share it with." [276] Companies such as Danone and Miyoko's Creamery will do well as investors focus on the nexus of food and climate security.

Pandemics

Should we categorize the COVID-19 pandemic and its associated economic and health destruction as a dislocation or a disruption? Whether a dislocation or a disruption, the moment showcased women as a critical pool of talent to meet the challenges in science, industry, and government. Globally, frontline health-care workers in many countries were 70% female, so women provided the care that everyone needed.[277]

Many countries led by women performed better at managing their citizens through the COVID-19 crisis than their male counterparts. Their empathetic leadership bolstered good behavior among the population, recognized and met people's economic and emotional needs, and emphasized strong and frequent communication. Female leadership prioritized saving lives and long-term economic safety over a fear of short-term costs. Women showed dynamic leadership that influenced passing legislation and issuing government orders quickly enough to meet the daily changes of the pandemic.

Women leaders in the private sector also performed well during the early stages of COVID-19. According to a *Harvard Business Review* survey of businesses across industries, women were stronger, more communicative leaders. During the pandemic, employees placed a premium on such interpersonal skills as "inspiring and motivating," "communicating powerfully," "collaboration/teamwork," and "relationship building." Women were rated higher than men on these skills in the survey of employees about their companies' leadership during the COVID-19 pandemic.[278]

The pandemic serves as an example of why female talent should be supported and promoted to leadership as often as male talent. As we discussed in chapter 1, female talent played a significant role in the scientific study of RNA (as opposed to focusing on DNA). What scientists know about RNA became critical to understanding how to develop vaccines for COVID-19 in an accelerated manner. Female scientists were involved in pioneering work in CRISPR gene editing that paved the way for the vaccines. We also know that developing and manufacturing the vaccines was the first hurdle. There were women in the labs, not all of whom have been recognized or rewarded for their groundbreaking research. Other female scientists' presence in the lab during the vaccine development helped establish trust in the vaccines from people who had reason not to trust that the vaccine would be safe.[279]

The opposite of the benefit of including women is the significant risk of not including them. Women who are close to problems are in the best position to find solutions. As we evolve toward the next economy, we have the framework to turn the crises of climate change, famine, and the pandemic into opportunities and to grow the pie to the benefit of all. For the next economy to fully accelerate, we will need to create a more stable world. But climate change and pandemics aren't the only obstacles to this. Other factors, including violent conflict, racial divisions, and gender-based violence, also contribute to destabilization.

Conflict

The 2016 Global Peace Index report found that in 2015, the economic impact of all violent conflicts (including war, homicide, incarceration, and police brutality) to the global economy was $13.6 trillion, equivalent to $5 per day for every person on the planet.[280] While there are fewer active wars around the world than there were in the period between 1960 and 2000, there are more active conflicts.[281] Ongoing conflict drives instability that in turn creates friction against economic growth. Unfortunately, many instances of conflict are fueled by a sense that the economic pie is shrinking. Territorial disputes have led to bloodshed in East Africa, the Middle East, Eastern Europe, and South and Southeast Asia. Resource-related disagreements are causing conflicts in Western Europe, Latin America, and even Antarctica. Ethnic and racial violence is occurring in the United States and across the globe, with every region experiencing its own form of conflict. In some instances, conflicts are expanding into wars, costing human lives and trillions of dollars that could instead be allocated to building better infrastructure or providing better health care and education.

But despite this bleak backdrop, we are optimistic about the possibilities for peace from including more voices in conflict resolution. Less war and violence can lead to better GDP growth outcomes at the macro level as well as better health and wealth outcomes at the individual level. Research shows that countries with higher levels of gender equality tend to have lower levels of conflict. Women provide a different way of managing conflict. In fact, data shows that including women in peace negotiations resulted in agreements that were 64% less likely to fail and 35% more likely to last at least 15 years.[282]

Racial Division

Conflict fueled by ethnic or racial divisions has increased in recent years. As the perception of a shrinking pie takes a stronger hold, people are becoming more tribal, ethnocentric, and concerned with amassing the most advantages for themselves and their kin. Such thinking is shortsighted because the challenges the world faces today do not discriminate in favor of a specific kind. While the systems behind our divisions might cause certain people to feel the pain more significantly in the short term, the connectedness of our lives has demonstrated that these artificial barriers cannot hold beyond a certain point.

By upholding tribal affiliations, we are perpetuating the education gaps, health gaps, and wealth gaps among communities. Globally, it is the North–South divide. Within countries, such divisions occur along class, religious, and racial groupings. Historically, we have not asked ourselves how our world could be different if we enabled everyone to develop their talents and apply them to innovation and economic activity. As smart and innovative as humans are, this is one experiment we have never run on a grand scale. The data that we do have supports the case for a full potential paradigm. Earlier we described the evidence that bringing women into full economic participation could result in an additional $28 trillion in global GDP growth, an increase of approximately 33% by 2025. Similarly, estimates indicate that closing the racial wealth gap in the United States by 2028 could increase US GDP by 4 to 6%.[283] For investors this means more assets under management, more capital to invest in profitable ventures, and the potential of greater individual wealth and health.

Gender-Based Violence

Gender-based violence (GBV), which usually targets women, is another global epidemic that harms the health and wealth of individuals, businesses, and societies at large. GBV cuts across all demographics and geographies; it occurs among family members and strangers. It knows no social or economic boundaries. Reduction of GBV around the globe is one of the best opportunities to grow the economic pie and improve the quality of life for all. According to a 2019 report from the World Bank, GBV affects one in three women in their lifetime.[284] In addition to the devastating physical and psychological impact on the survivors of violence and their families, GBV also generates huge social and economic costs. The World Bank estimates that in some countries, GBV shrinks GDP by as much as

3.7%.[285] According to UN Women, women in India lose an average of at least five paid workdays for each incident of intimate partner violence.[286] Annual costs of intimate partner violence have been calculated at $5.8 billion in the United States, $1.16 billion in Canada, and $11.38 billion in Australia.[287] Estimates show GBV is a leading cause of homicide and exacts significantly higher economic costs than non-GBV-related homicides or civil wars. GBV has a huge negative impact on women's participation in the workforce, education, and civic life, and it drains resources from social services, health-care systems, and businesses.[288]

Knowing all of this, why don't businesses and governments put a higher priority on reducing GBV? Given the huge toll on the health and wealth of our societies and individuals, why don't governments and financial systems apply the same type of "all hands on deck" mentality to decreasing it as they have to developing COVID-19 vaccines? After all, if GBV is allowed to persist in our families and societies, all our efforts to grow the pie and expand our economies will be undermined.

We must begin to address this epidemic as a preventable health issue. Currently, the systems that need to be changed to drive a reduction in violence (such as health care, research, education, urban planning, safety, and crime enforcement) have insufficient numbers of women in leadership to accurately represent women's needs. We need a shift in perspective to tackle this scourge. What would it look like if the people who are most often the victims of GBV (women and girls) were the ones enlisted to solve it?

In chapter 1 we described examples showing when women are given the resources to address the problem of violence in their communities, they can have a dramatic impact on the prevalence and the consequences. But both men and women need to prioritize the reduction in GBV in order to allow for the economic growth and stability of our businesses and societies. This is another example of an investable opportunity. When women have access to financial resources that allow them to innovate and solve problems, they generate tremendous return on investment.

WHY NOW? THE RISK OF DELAY

What are the risks of the status quo? As a society, we will leave value and capacity on the table if we ignore the changing economy and the roles that women can play. Innovative solutions will lag the dislocations and disruptions that are already happening or are nearby. We see this in the United States when legislators push back against defining infrastructure as something more than just roads and bridges. If more people work from home and no longer rely on transportation to get to an office or factory to be productive, then infrastructure must include all the things that allow everyone in the workforce to be successful while working from home, such as functional Internet services and childcare.

In *Peers Inc,* her book about the founding of Zipcar, Robin Chase discusses the value of excess capacity.[289] In the Zipcar story, value was created by changing car ownership to a sharing model to take advantage of underutilized capacity. In the post-pandemic economy, leaders and workers who can't do their jobs because they don't have reliable Internet or childcare represent underutilized capacity. At a societal level, the risk of waiting also manifests in the decreased productivity of those large public companies that do not take the needs of their diverse workforce into consideration. Disruptive social movements such as #MeToo and Black Lives Matter, coupled with the public's expectation for corporate transparency, have hurt many otherwise successful organizations that failed to address the valid concerns of these social movements.

What are the risks of waiting on an individual level? If you are reading this book and have a role in making financial decisions (whether as a CEO, government official, board member, investment advisor, venture capitalist, entrepreneur, or consumer), you must involve and consider women in your decisions or you will miss an opportunity for stronger financial performance. The newest generation of leaders expects diversity and sees the value of collaboration in professional decision-making. Those who do not adapt to this new total talent paradigm will have a lesser role in growing the economic pie, and they will earn a smaller piece of it.

We also must consider the risk of losing women from the workforce. The COVID-19 pandemic showed what can happen to society when we encounter significant disruptions and dislocations. In rich countries, with the onset of lockdowns, the traditional work day changed very quickly. The 6:30 a.m. alarm would no longer signal that it was time for parents to get up, dress their kids, make lunches, drop kids off at the bus or school, drive to work, put in an eight-hour day with colleagues, struggle to leave work on time to pick up kids from after-school programs, stop at the grocery store, and then go home for an evening of dinner, homework, and a little TV before bed. In March 2020, the alarm might still have gone off at 6:30 a.m., but the daily middle-class routines now included making sure the Wi-Fi could support four simultaneous Zoom calls, identifying the few remaining online sources to buy toilet paper, and fighting over who was going to train the new pandemic puppy. Other changes and reconfigurations happened in every community around the world. The burden of illness (from COVID-19 and the neglect of preventive care), surges in domestic violence, and increases in obesity and addiction during the pandemic have been well documented. We also saw the disproportionate economic impact on women from temporary shrinking economies.

A primary driver of this comes from the imbalance in household responsibilities between men and women. The 2020 UN Women rapid gender assessment on the impact of COVID-19 indicates that it widened existing gaps in the amount of time women spend on household chores and caregiving. This impacts not just women but girls as well (because families may be relying on daughters to combat increased workloads).[290] In its recent report, "Women in the Workplace 2020," McKinsey & Company found that since the pandemic, mothers who are part of dual-career households were likely to spend more than five additional hours per day on household chores.[291] This extra work is on top of the pre-pandemic burden of unpaid care work that is typical for the female workforce. Women have thus suffered a disproportionate impact on their economic security because they've been forced to make the difficult decision to abandon their jobs as their uncompensated home caregiving work increases.

To add to the misery, McKinsey & Company reported that fewer than a third of companies surveyed adjusted their performance-review criteria to account for the increase in demands from home on their female workforce.[292] And very few governments have addressed the increased burdens of domestic work and care work in their COVID-19 relief measures. These forces have caused women to burn out and leave the workforce at a faster pace than men.[293] Women have also taken on the brunt of frontline stress, given that 70% of essential care workers are female. The lack of governmental investment in those sectors resulted in women leaving these jobs and a shortage of care workers around the world. In September 2020, four times as many women as men left the US labor force, and a quarter of the women who lost their jobs during the pandemic cited a lack of childcare as the biggest reason—twice as many as men.[294]

This trend is true for more than lower-level workers. The McKinsey report also noted that women in leadership positions are held to the pre-pandemic performance expectations under pandemic conditions. They have more scrutiny and higher standards placed on them—especially if they are the only woman on the team. According to the report, women in leadership are 50% more likely than men in senior leadership to consider changing jobs, downshifting their roles (fewer hours or responsibilities, losing out on critical career development), or leaving the workforce altogether. In a survey of senior executive women, three-quarters of respondents pointed to burnout as the primary cause for such considerations.[295]

Throughout history, when women have entered the workforce in significant numbers, GDP, economic productivity, the value of the private sector, and stock prices have increased. As we stated earlier, a pre-pandemic report in

2017 from S&P Global estimated that the US economy would have grown by an additional $1.6 trillion if women entered and stayed in the workforce at rates similar to those in Norway, where caregiving is compensated through a combination of corporate-funded benefits and government-funded programs.[296] In our review of the literature, we found many other studies that demonstrate a significant correlation between the rate of female labor participation and strong economic development.

Remote work presents a new opportunity for employers and employees, men and women alike, to allow for increased flexibility of time and the breakdown of space barriers, and thus the maximization of talent. However, if we are not paying attention to how the demands of the home are met (usually by women, especially during COVID-19), this opportunity might turn into a massive loss of talent—that of women. If companies and governments react well and use this opportunity to build a more flexible, empathetic, family-friendly workplace cocreated by the women who are closest to the problems that need to be solved, the most talented employees will be retained and hired, resulting in healthier and wealthier communities. Furthermore, this will create a nurturing culture that will allow more women equal opportunities to reach their full potential—and end up with a stronger, more dynamic workforce.

The success of the next economy will depend on employers being nimble and flexible in how they support their workers. Rather than letting essential and valuable workers abandon their posts, they need to retain that talent and focus on bringing new, inclusive talent into the market and allowing that talent to reshape the world. Investors can drive this change by investing in companies that under-stand and implement this imperative.

THE BOTTOM LINE

Savvy investors who anticipate the dislocations and disruptions in the next economy will make better returns with lower risk. Investments that utilize diverse talent to create the innovation and solutions to the problems ahead of us will be more profitable and will contribute to the expansion of the economic pie.

CHAPTER 4
MATERIAL RISKS
OF INACTION

I N THIS SECTION WE WILL FOCUS ON THE MATERIAL risks to investments if women are not included in portfolio management, whether investments are in companies, funds, or countries. Some of these risks come in the form of opportunity costs (i.e., the loss of potential gain from other alternatives when one alternative is selected). These missed opportunities include failures to transition from unstable governments, to identify the most innovative early stage companies, to retain the best workforce, or to take full advantage of the enormous female consumer market. Whether you are an investor in the sovereign bond market, a venture capital fund, or a consumer products company, the lack of female talent at executive levels represents a significant material risk to your financial returns. As we have seen in previous chapters, female participation and leadership mitigate the instability that can take a tremendous toll and undermine the success of enterprises.

At the macro level, including women in the leadership of countries creates more stable operating environments and thriving citizens who feel more secure and are more open to collaboration, which lead to more productivity. In a comparable way, at the level of companies, growing the numbers of women in leadership representation or investing in female workforce-retention efforts creates a more committed company culture and a more stable business. We recognize that diversifying talent comes with costs, including the costs of talent acquisition and training. However, these costs are limited compared to the more significant and long-term costs of exclusion. The status quo of limited inclusion of female talent in most governing bodies and companies today not only interferes with the positive outcomes we detailed in the previous sections but also is a risk that undermines operations, profitability, growth, and the stability of governance.

In addition to these opportunity costs, material risks to enterprises also cause direct and indirect financial damage to individuals, companies, and economies. As you'll see in the upcoming chapter, these direct financial costs can be quantified. But indirect costs from a lack of female talent can also accrue across numerous dimensions, including the impact of poor health, crime, poverty, and many other dimensions that interfere with the quality of our lives. While these indirect costs are harder to quantify, they can result in overall headwinds on societies, inhibiting economic growth and stability. Examples of such material risks include the impact of sexual harassment in the workplace and the failure of societies to cover the provision of reproductive and maternal health care to their female workers. Sadly, the world has been experiencing these headwinds at a more accelerated rate. These indirect costs affect both the people who are making the financial decisions and those who are excluded from them. Those excluded may suffer the impact of lost wages, poor nutrition, and increased violence. Those who have traditionally been included in financial decision-making also suffer—in their case from stress-induced conditions borne out of the anxiety of protecting their share of the pie.[297] Undoubtedly, an operating model that is more inclusive would serve all of society better. Let's look at some examples of how failing to include female talent in financial decision-making puts your investments at risk.

RISKS FROM GOVERNMENT INSTABILITY
In previous sections of the book, we discussed specific female traits and differences in leadership style that contribute to strong positive outcomes in financial performance and, in the case of female political leaders, to the general stability of governments. There is a financial cost to investing in unstable places and a financial upside to investing in secure and stable countries. In this section we elaborate on specific country-level risks of not having female leaders or male leaders who have the traits exhibited by female leaders. We are making this case to shed light on the economic value of female leadership styles at a country level and to present the case for investors to direct capital to enterprises within countries that are more stable or purchase these countries' sovereign debt.

In February 2020 the Global Soft Power Index outlined the soft (female) power traits as being communicative, flexible, and patient, contrasting with hard (male) power qualities that include aggression and control. It was not designed as an investable index, but we argue that it could be used judiciously to influence investment decisions. It has several limitations to be useful as a real index, including the small sample size for women-led countries compared to male-led countries, but the data reveals patterns that cannot be ignored by investors who want to reduce risk through managing macro instability, which sometimes leads to micro-level volatility.[298]

The study covered a sample of over 55,000 respondents, including specialists and the public, in 100 countries. It reviewed broad variables that, combined, provide a view of a country's "presence, reputation, and impact on the world stage."[299] These included country brands that are characterized by soft power being more positively "memorable," the overall positive or negative influence and reputation of a country on the world stage, and performance across seven "Soft Power Pillars" (business and trade, governance, international relations, culture and heritage, media and communication, education and science, and people and values).[300] For us, a key takeaway from the study is that although nations governed by men are considered to have more influence overall, they are also seen to have a far more negative influence on average than their counterparts with female leadership. Those female-led counterparts, on the other hand, enjoy better reputations around the world. Most of the strong performances are within three key themes of safety and security, trust and ethics, and stability. These attributes lead to outperformance in governance, international relations, and business and trade, among other categories. After the way the world experienced and witnessed female leadership during the 2020 start of the pandemic (recall the research cited earlier indicating female-led governments performed better relative to male-led governments in their COVID-19 pandemic management), it is reasonable to assume that there may be fewer skeptics around the governance and international relations spheres. Some readers may be surprised to find business and trade on this list—after all, men are generally believed to be better business leaders. But we are not surprised at all. This is another example of female leadership having a direct positive impact on business performance.[301]

The study found that the leaders of most countries exhibit leadership styles that lead to conflict. Some countries have strong institutions and regulatory regimes that buffer some of the downside risk from these leaders, but others do not. Investing into these economies presents real financial risks in the form of lost profits, lost business, failed businesses, or the need to have political risk insurance coverage (defined as a tool for businesses to manage risks arising from the adverse actions—or inactions—of governments).[302]

Political risk insurance, traditionally provided by government agencies, has been a way to reduce risks for businesses directly investing in and trading with more-volatile countries. Since the 1970s, political risk insurance has grown into a lucrative business, involving both private and public insurance companies, as more investors consider it essential protection when facing the risks of moving capital into unstable markets. Broker Willis Towers Watson's 2019 survey of 41 major corporations found that 61% of those companies considered political risk levels to have increased from 2018 and 68% of the 41 corporations had seen losses due to political risks. Among those 68% that had seen losses, 32% with revenues exceeding $1 billion had seen a catastrophic political risk loss of $250 million or more.[303]

Other evaluators have come to the same conclusion about the world's political climate. Allianz SE, a financial services company based in Munich, observed in 2021 that political risks and violence were in the top 10 major risks included in the Allianz Risk Barometer for the first time since 2018, with civil unrest, protests, and riots now posing risk to companies comparable to risks of terrorism. Losses from such events were particularly pronounced in 2019–2020, including $90 million from France's "yellow vest" protests, $77 million from unrest in Hong Kong, $821 million from unrest in Ecuador, and $2 billion from unrest in Chile prior to the adoption of its new constitutional committee.[304] The United States has not been immune to such turmoil; with the rise of both social justice–driven events on one end and civil disorder events such as the 2021 Capitol riots on the other, the United States rose from 91st to 34th on the Verisk Maplecroft Civil Unrest Index of riskiest jurisdictions.[305]

In another related measure of government stability attributed to female leadership, Goldman Sachs reported in 2021 on their success investing in government bonds in emerging markets that score higher on a gender-equality index. Their research outlines a winning bond strategy based on an economy's success on women's education, labor, health, agency, and power. "A portfolio of debt from the eight developing economies with the best track records of empowering women would have outperformed the eight with the worst by about 1% over the past seven years."[306] The researchers noted that the improved performance was especially pronounced during times of market volatility, not unlike the times we face today and the disruptions and dislocations ahead of us. Once again, we see that screening investment opportunities for gender will bring higher returns and less risk.

RISKS FROM NATURAL DISASTERS

We should also consider the costs associated with investing in communities that have repeated occurrences of natural disasters, or *force majeure* events. *Force majeure* is a French term that is translated as "superior force." In law and business in most jurisdictions, this clause allows contracting parties not to hold each other accountable for losses when performance under a contract is not possible due to circumstances beyond the control of the parties. As natural disasters become more frequent, should investors take measures to mitigate these risks as well as making investments into innovations that address the risks?

Per new scientific findings released in the 2021 UN IPCC Global Climate Report, severe weather events tied to climate change may lead to more frequent invocation of force majeure clauses, thereby disrupting more business deals and projects and introducing greater inefficiency to the market as a whole.[307] As such severe events become more commonplace, the increase in force majeure clauses may push courts to reinterpret force majeure to no longer include certain climate events. Business partners would thus have to shoulder the financial burden for losses themselves, costing them credibility with their investors and business profits.

As the need to properly evaluate risk becomes more important, women must be included in financial decision-making. As discussed in earlier sections, women are more oriented toward long-term risk evaluation, more aware of risks, and more interested in making investments that address these risks. It is likely that a transition to curtail the scope of force majeure clauses will happen sooner rather than later. Emerging regulatory reform movements seek to limit the scope of force majeure clauses, making it harder for contracting parties to get out of performance or liability in the event of a natural catastrophe, especially in the case of crises that have become increasingly common.[308]

RISKS INHERENT IN THE STATUS QUO

As we have noted in previous chapters, women are too often excluded from enterprise-level and fund-management decision-making. In seed investing, which involves small funds for early-stage companies, women are investing at a participation rate of 22%, as reported in a 2017 report from Wharton Business School and Harvard Business School.[309] As minimum investment sizes become larger, such as with venture capital, the number of women investors shrinks considerably. The same report indicated that women represent 5 to 8% of investors in venture capital, which is critical to innovation and economic growth.[310] This limited participation has significant consequences given venture capital's growing impact on the American economy specifically and the world broadly.

Venture-funded companies often take up significant space in the global economy. In a study published in 2015, two Stanford University researchers reviewed the impact of venture investing and reported that many venture-backed companies have fueled the US economy, and thereby the global economy, over the last thirty years, including Google, FedEx, and Intel. As of 2015, one-fifth of US public companies were venture-backed.[311] And in 2022, seven of the world's most valuable companies by market cap—Apple, Amazon, Alphabet (Google), Microsoft, Facebook, Alibaba, and Tencent—were venture backed.[312]

Even though the number of female venture capitalists is increasing (of the 5.6% of US venture capital (VC) firms led by women, more than 70% were founded in the last five years), the absolute numbers remain extraordinarily low.[313] Only 4.9% of VC partners in the United States are women.[314] A 2018 *Harvard Business Review* report noted that VC firms that increased the number of female partners by 10% experienced a 1.5% increase in fund returns each year, plus 9.7% more of their exits were profitable.[315] The opportunity cost of not including women in venture capital decisions is not just in missed financial returns but in the selection of companies that are funded and thereby given the financial fuel to grow and provide value to our lives. VC firms are missing out on investing in early stage companies that are innovating essential products and services (think mRNA). Oftentimes it takes gender-diverse teams to translate innovation—especially innovation developed by women—to commercialization. A 2019 All Raise report showed that female funders are two times more likely to invest in start-ups with one female founder and more than three times more likely to invest in companies with a female CEO.[316]

When space is not made for women in existing VC firms, smart women must create that space for themselves, a significant undertaking of time and treasure that pulls them out of the game while they build. We know investors are most likely to invest in enterprises that are led by individuals who look most like themselves. By not having diversity on the team making the investment decisions, many potentially extraordinary companies led by diverse talent will never be considered for investments.[317]

RISKS FROM LOST TALENT

When talented individuals decide to leave a company, there is a cost that includes the missed return on investment in that talent, the loss of intellectual capital that would have led to competitive advantage, and the cost of acquiring new talent. Savvy investors choose companies that have stable work-forces and low attrition statistics. Internal instability is costly; replacing workers costs on average 33% of the salary of the lost talent. According to a 2017 Network of Executive Women survey of more than 3,600 US employees in the retail and consumer goods industry, women reported leaving their jobs at higher rates than men—31% versus 24%.[318] The numbers are more extreme as women move up the corporate ladder, where women leave at rates that are three times higher than male colleagues.[319] These statistics indicate that companies must do more to retain their female staff, including equal pay for equal work and creating working environments that value women. The research outlined a number of reasons women leave at higher percentages, including (1) burnout, given the challenges women face when making their ways up the corpo-rate ladder and finding themselves in rooms where they are in a minority and facing greater scrutiny; (2) more challenging work environments; and (3) having to pay for more personal infrastructure, including childcare, while on average making less money compared to their male colleagues.[320]

In the financial sector, the starting numbers for women are low so any attrition has an even larger impact. In invest-ment banking, women represent less than 17% of senior leadership, in private equity 9%, and at hedge funds and private debt firms 11%.[321] These are essential parts of the economy that influence where capital flows. These are people who decide which sovereign bonds to buy, which corporate bonds to invest in, which companies will receive equity and debt capital, and so on. The dismal numbers of female participation and attrition in these positions exacts a significant cost on society. Investors and companies with policies and practices that not only enable their female talent to stay but also reward them for doing so are the ones that will perform better in the long term.

RISKS TO PRODUCTS AND SERVICES

Earlier, we looked at some examples of the financial, social, and human costs of not having women at product design tables in areas such as auto safety and heart disease prevention. In addition, too many companies design their products and services without incorporating the needs of female consumers. There are material risks in lost revenue to these companies and to the overall economy when women's needs are not considered.

In 2020, women made up more than half of the population of the United States and controlled or influenced 85% of consumer spending. This includes over 90% of the consumer decision-making for new homes, vacations, bank accounts, food, and over-the-counter pharmaceuticals. It has been estimated that worldwide, women control over $31.8 trillion in spending.[322] And yet "91% of women feel that advertisers don't understand them."[323] In 2016, *Fast Company* reported "a large percentage of products and services across various industries are not satisfying women. Women are the primary decision-makers for 85% of car purchases, but 74% of women feel they are misunderstood by the automotive industry. Women make 80% of household health decisions, but 66% of women feel misunderstood by health-care marketers. Women over the age of 50 control more than half of all discretionary income in the United States, but 53% feel ignored by brands."[324]

In 2009, Michael Silverstein and Kate Sayre from the Boston Consulting Group reported in *Harvard Business Review* on the results of a market survey of more than 12,000 women from all over the world and from a variety of socio-economic levels. They found that "women feel vastly under-served . . . and undervalued in the marketplace and under-estimated in the workplace." They went on to summarize that "few companies have responded to [women's] need for time-saving solutions or for products and services designed specifically for them. . . . Although women control spending in most categories of consumer goods, too many businesses behave as if they had no say over purchasing decisions." Silverstein and Sayre conclude that the potential growth market of female consumers is bigger than that of China and India combined.[325]

In her book *Winning Her Business*, Bridget Brennan emphasizes that female consumers have what she calls a "multiplier effect." By this she means that even when women aren't paying for something with their own money, they often have a strong influence in purchasing decisions—whether it's within their families or at work. And if a woman is making decisions on behalf of her coworkers, spouse, or children, the choices she makes are likely to have a ripple effect and "multiply" within these communities. This means that when women buy products for other people, these other people are then likely to continue purchasing these products in the future. Women are more likely to share their purchasing decisions with their friends. This multiplier effect means that one happy female customer translates into many other satisfied customers (both male and female). Brennan also emphasizes that companies that have women leading their design, sales, or senior management teams will successfully market to women.[326]

While the failure of companies to market to women exists across all industries, of particular interest to readers of this book may be the risk to the financial services industry if it does not effectively take care of female customers. As reported by Silverstein and Sayre in *Harvard Business Review*, 93% of women say they have considerable influence on what financial services their family purchases, yet this industry is notorious for failing to take women's needs into account. As Silverstein and Sayre write, "Financial Services wins the prize as the industry least sympathetic to women—and one in which companies stand to gain the most if they can change their approach."[327]

The Internet is full of articles describing how 70 to 90% of newly widowed women leave their family's financial advisor within a year of their husband's death.[328] Financial advisors who don't adjust their services to meet the needs of women are leaving trillions of dollars on the table.

RISKS FROM SEXUAL HARASSMENT

Sexual harassment is defined by the Equal Opportunity Commission as follows: "Unwelcome sexual advances, requests for sexual favors, and other verbal or physical conduct of a sexual nature constitute sexual harassment when (a) submission to such conduct is made either explicitly or implicitly a term or condition of an individual's employment, (b) submission to or rejection of such conduct by an individual is used as the basis for employment decisions affecting such individual, or (c) such conduct has the purpose or effect of unreasonably interfering with an individual's work performance, or creating an intimidating, hostile, or offensive work environment."[329]

In 2016, the Equal Employment Opportunity Commission estimated that up to 85% of US women have experienced sexual harassment issues at work.[330] A typical Fortune 500 company loses $14 million a year from sexual assault settlements, and for the federal government, that figure is $327 million a year.[331] The direct costs of sexual harassment certainly include the direct expense of legal claims but also include the cost of employee turnover and loss of revenue from advertising and brand destruction.

In 2020, the *Journal of Corporate Finance* published a study that investigated the impact of a sexual harassment scandal on the share price of a public company. Researchers saw an approximately 1.5% abnormal decrease in the value of a company on the day of the news coverage and the following trading day—with the impact amplified by an additional 5% drop in value if the CEO is involved in the incident.[332]

Another study, published in 2021 by Social Science Research Network (SSRN), investigated the impact of job reviews posted by rank-and-file employees regarding harassment in their workplaces. The authors concluded sexual harassment (SH) "reveals significant future problems for firms in terms of profitability, labor costs, and stock performance. . . . High SH scores are associated with sharp declines in operating profitability and increases in labor costs. Firms in the top quantiles (top 1% to 5%) of the SH score earned lower risk-adjusted stock returns, representing an annual shareholder value loss of $0.8 to $1.4 billion per harassment-prone firm. These results indicate that sexual harassment claims are highly correlated with firm value, and employee voluntary reporting can be a valid disclosure mechanism when firms are disincentivized to reveal bad news."[333] In other words, when the leadership of a company tries to minimize or cover up a sexual harassment situation, individual employees can provide the public disclosure with expensive consequences to the company.

But even before the #MeToo movement and the very public shaming of CEOs, politicians, and others, sexual harassment took its financial toll on businesses through lost productivity, absenteeism (short-term absences from work, including sick leave, annual leave, and unpaid leave), presenteeism (reduced productivity while at work), staff turnover, and management time spent processing complaints. In March 2019, Deloitte published a review of the economic costs of sexual harassment in the workplace. They investigated the indirect costs of SH and concluded that "the economic costs of workplace sexual harassment are shared by individuals, their employers, government, and society. Approximately 70% of lost revenue is borne by employers, with the government losing 23% of tax revenue and individuals losing 7% of income. Between the sub-groups, most of the per person productivity losses are due to differences in income in each group."[334] Over time, workplace sexual harassment has an enormous public health impact in the form of chronic depression, post-traumatic stress disorder, sleep disorders, and other mental health issues.[335]

What can investors do to avoid investments in companies that haven't adequately prevented workplace sexual harassment and its associated direct and indirect costs?

A place to start would be to check if companies in your portfolio require harassment training. Many US states and foreign countries require some sort of harassment training in the workforce.[336] Reports show employees who undergo trainings are more aware of sexual harassment and that awareness can result in an increase in reporting. It also can be effective in mobilizing bystanders to intervene and result in culture change within the workplace. However, workplace sexual harassment training programs by themselves are unlikely to decrease the incidence of sexual harassment or reduce the cost to businesses. For training programs or other types of interventions to be effective, there must be support from the very top of an organization.[337] In other words, without leadership at a company, an increase in awareness, reporting, and changing culture by themselves won't result in an actual decrease in harassment or protect the company from the costs of harassment.

What about hiring more women in leadership positions? A study from 2020 that looked at the number of sexual harassment claims in the workforce on college campuses found that having more women in the upper administration of the university or college has a significant correlation to fewer harassment claims. But without the support of other women in upper administration, simply having a woman as president was not helpful. The study found a single woman at the top made no significant difference but a *team* of women at the top as part of the administration did noticeably reduce sexual harassment in the academic workplace.[338] Another study published in 2020 found companies with more female board directors or more women in senior leadership had fewer sexual harassment claims.[339]

It appears as if the most effective way to decrease the cost of sexual harassment in the workplace is to have a higher representation of female managers and to have more equal power distribution between men and women.[340] This is one more example of how sharing leadership and financial decision-making with women results in cost savings for organizations. Ultimately, if investors demand female leadership within their portfolio companies, it will decrease the costs of sexual harassment.

RISKS FROM POOR ACCESS TO REPRODUCTIVE HEALTH

Many readers may be wondering about the connection between women's financial leadership, reproductive health, and financial returns. Currently, most businesses don't see the connection between reproductive health and a healthy workforce. However, for businesses to optimize women's talents, women must be able to fully participate in the workforce. This means women must have easy access to family planning to control when and how they have children. Simply put, it is not possible for companies to succeed in building a diverse and inclusive workforce without policies that support employees accessing comprehensive reproductive health care and family planning, fertility management, quality maternal health care, and caregiving services after delivery.[341] Women who have access to the health care they need to manage approximately three decades of fertility with minimal complications are healthier, have healthier children (if they choose to have children), use fewer costly health-care services, and remain in the workforce.[342]

Business leadership that is more inclusive of female talent recognizes that reproductive health is a business imperative.

These needs are particularly acute given the setbacks to workforce participation by women that have resulted from the pandemic.[343] We were shown in 2020 that women's employment is more vulnerable to social pressures such as a disruption of childcare or needing to take care of sick family members. Unplanned pregnancies or pregnancy complications add an additional stress that can be the incident that forces women to leave the workforce. Furthermore, among developed countries, the United States has the highest rate of people dying of pregnancy-related complications during or within twelve months of the end of pregnancy.[344] And the death rates are getting worse, not better. According to the National Institutes of Health, the US maternal death rate in 2000 was 18.8 deaths per 100,000 live births. That rate has increased to 23.8 deaths per 100,000 live births in 2014.[345]

Restrictions on access to reproductive health care and suboptimized maternal health are at cross purposes with such stated corporate values as equity and inclusion and also affect the ability of economies and businesses to deliver on their value propositions. After the passage of Senate Bill 8 in Texas, which outlaws abortions after six weeks of pregnancy, a public opinion poll reported that 66% of college-educated workers (58% of men and 74% of women respondents) would not take a job in a state that prohibits abortions.[346] This is a huge risk to companies with significant workforces in Texas. Jim Doyle, president of Business Forward Foundation, was quoted in *Forbes* as saying, "Helping women succeed at work is the biggest lever we have to grow the economy."[347] At the national level in the United States, new research from the Institute for Women's Policy Research (IWPR) estimates that if, for instance, all of the damaging state-level restrictions on abortion were eliminated, an additional 505,000 women would enter the labor force. If this additional workforce made the same wages as similar women in their state, there would be an additional $3 billion dollars annually added to wages that would go back to the state's economy.[348]

Employers win when they prioritize positive maternal health outcomes. One comprehensive analysis found that for every dollar spent on family planning care, $1.60 is saved in maternal care costs. Other studies have shown that a dollar invested can save as much as $5.19. Cost savings result from the reduced rate of hospitalizations among infants born to mothers who received quality maternal health care.[349] Other drivers of poor outcomes and excessive costs associated with pregnancy and birth include unnecessary cesarean sections, preterm births, and high turnover rates associated with insufficient workplace support. These costs are compounded by the need to return to work as a top reason new mothers cite for ending breastfeeding. The benefits of breastfeeding to both mother and child are so profound that the American Academy of Pediatrics and the World Health Organization recommend that all infants breastfeed exclusively for their first six months.[350] Women who know that their work environment is compatible with their breastfeeding goals are less likely to be absent from work and less likely to quit, thereby reducing the high cost of turnover and lost productivity.[351]

What must investors do to prevent the harm to their investments from restrictive reproductive health policies and inadequate maternal health policies? Many might think that they have no control over these policies, as they are usually enacted through highly political government actions. But investors and businesses have plenty of opportunities to influence and protect their investments. First, they can choose to invest in countries and states that have more equitable laws that guarantee access to services for all communities. Investors can also demand that the companies in which they already own equity adopt or maintain inclusive policies for reproductive health access, safe maternal health care, and breastfeeding. This is especially true in the United States, where private and public companies dictate the quality of health-care coverage for their employees. And there are opportunities for all individuals to consider the impact of the political candidates they support, either through financial contributions (both at the individual and corporate level) or through the ballot box. While some politicians might describe themselves as "business friendly," if they support legislation that restricts access to reproductive health services, they are not business friendly at all.

THE BOTTOM LINE

There are enormous financial benefits from women's financial leadership and innovation decisions—benefits that show up as better performance and financial rewards across investments in all asset classes. Furthermore, inaction poses material risks to investments, including lost opportunities and direct and indirect financial costs. In the next section, we will see what the world will look like when a total talent paradigm is used to redesign some essential sectors, including the "care economy," health care, the environment, and wealth management.

CHAPTER 5

INVESTOR ROAD MAPS FOR FUTURE ECONOMIES

NVESTORS WILL OPTIMIZE RETURNS ON THEIR PORTFO-
lios from investments that prioritize female talent.
What will these portfolios look like when women are
fully engaged in tackling some of the biggest economic,
environmental, and social challenges in the world? How
can investors be prepared to take full advantage of investing
in the ensuing innovations and solutions? Women have
mostly been excluded from the financial decision-making
that impacts economies and markets—yet they are the
ones who are most proximate to the dysfunctions and inefficiencies that currently exist. Let's review what the care
economy, health care, environmental, and wealth management sectors look like when women share in the financial
decision-making and leadership. If you are an investor, you
are lucky to be reading this section of the book. We have
provided sample checklists in each section to include as part
of your investment and due diligence process.

CARE ECONOMY
A 2021 report from Pivotal Ventures identified that childcare contributes $648 billion to the US economy. The care
economy includes far more than the cost of childcare. It also
includes "tech for new parents, early education programs,
household management like laundry and cleaning to aging-
in-place services and long-term-care insurance."[352] As it
exists now, the care economy is a dysfunctional market.
Classic economic supply and demand theory has not led
to appropriate market pricing of talent. Instead, cultural
norms inform pricing. In this section we will discuss how
the sector will provide extensive investment opportunities
when women are at the table to drive decisions, including

financial decisions, in the care economy. We present the status quo and then describe what could be as the world navigates toward the next economy. Addressing the issues endemic in the care economy requires long-term thinking, innovation from the most proximate actors, and collaboration among individuals across different spheres of the economy—all characteristics of female leadership.

Today's care economy is disproportionally female, underpaid, and suffering from underinvestment. Women represent 94% of the early childhood care and education workforce and 87.7% of the health care and care support workforce.[353] They also undertake more than three-quarters of unpaid care work in the world. As a result of unequal share of domestic responsibilities, it is estimated that 42% of women in the world cannot participate in paid work due to caretaking responsibilities, compared to only 6% of men.[354] And despite a growing demand for care services and recognition of the critical importance of care services to economic growth, most caregivers do not have access to decent living wages and benefits. One in six US caregivers reports living in poverty, while 90% of the world's domestic workers lack any type of social welfare protection from their governments.[355]

Care work is currently predominantly female. What if it were professionalized to promote equal participation across genders? Care work is under-remunerated. What if it were remunerated at a rate that correlated with the value it provides to the economy? Childcare is too expensive. What if it were made less expensive through innovative entrepreneurial offerings, employer providers, state-supported centers, and community-run co-ops? Eldercare is too expensive. What if it were made less expensive through the same opportunities as early childcare? In the next section we review examples of markets that have innovated and implemented solutions, creating better health and wealth for individuals and communities.

Women's control of financial decisions in the care economy will result in better market forces coming into play, and these market forces will influence value recognition, gender redistribution of responsibilities, and market-based remuneration.

"I don't think anybody does a better job than mothers in the home, and any bill that makes it easier or more convenient for mothers to come out of the home and let others raise their child, I don't think that's a good direction for us to be going," said Idaho state representative Charlie Shepherds during the discussion of a bill on the Idaho House floor. "We are really hurting the family unit in the process."[356] This statement is notable because it was made in March 2021 by a member of a state governing body, in one of the most developed countries in the world, and it runs counter to the assumption that cultural issues around care work are a third-world challenge. The cultural norms around care work prevail everywhere, in varying degrees of market-distorting levels. The statement tells us much about one of the causes of the dysfunction in the care economy around the world and across its entire value chain: from early childhood care to eldercare and every type of care work in between, most societies operate with the expectation that such work is a duty that is primarily female. So long as this cultural norm stands, much care work will not be recognized as professional work. It will continue to be undervalued, underpaid, and a missed investment opportunity. A different paradigm in the care economy would value care work, create opportunities for more market-oriented innovations, and present an investable universe of solutions. According to a 2018 report by the International Labor Organization, such a market-based approach could potentially lead to the creation of an estimated 269 million jobs globally if investments in education, health, and social work doubled by 2030.[357]

The great news is that systemic change in the care work sector will happen when investors recognize the business opportunities. Innovators abound, and smart people are always looking for areas to disrupt. One need only look at technological disruptions in the last couple of decades by companies such as Zipcar, Airbnb, and Lyft—companies that saw opportunities to disrupt the travel and transportation industry and thereby create new jobs and whole new economies. The bad news for the potential of the care economy is that cultural norms that stand in the way of market forces can be the toughest knots to untangle. Nevertheless, the pandemic and the disruption in childcare for working families has highlighted the need for effective services for everyone. Soon, savvy investors will see the potential for change and a shift in investor perceptions of the potential for strategic investments and strong returns. Patience has witnessed this shift in the emerging trend in investor communities focused on generating a care economy investment pipeline. More strategic investors collaborating with Women of the World Endowment are building care economy investment pipelines.

More people, male and female, spent 2020 working from home—learning how to be "in the office" from home, juggling stepping in as homeschool teachers for their young children or eldercare managers for their aging parents. Currently there is a more universal view of the value of care work and therefore the potential to move beyond norms and address the what-if questions. Women, who have traditionally been most proximate to providing care, will lead the change in this area, collaborating with male partners who, thanks to the pandemic, have had the experience of caregiving.

In our post-pandemic world, we have an opportunity for a change in basic assumptions and true systemic change of the care economy. Care work has long been inadequately remunerated, and numerous studies have concluded that one of the major reasons for this is the fact that caregivers are mostly female. Millions of homes across the world have mothers who are both the main caregiver and the main breadwinner of the family, yet the undervaluation of care work has not shifted. Some of these women are caregivers for their own families in an unremunerated capacity and caregivers for other families in an under-remunerated capacity, leading to cycles of poverty. In the United States, women spend 37% more time on household and care work than male counterparts.[358] When care work is recognized as valuable and compensated at market levels, it will be distributed across genders, it will be more balanced, and we will have greater innovation and more capital directed at care work innovations.

The question we must ask is whether the challenges would be so endemic if the cultural norm that defines care work as female did not interfere with market forces and if the care economy were equally attractive both to female and male workers. The answer is no, to put it bluntly; if men did more care work, we would have higher pay and greater allocation of investor capital.

Between an aging population that increasingly requires eldercare and the COVID-19 pandemic that disrupted the school system as part of caregiving infrastructure for families with young children, it has become obvious that care work is essential to the well-being of communities, businesses, and economies. Investing in the care economy is not only critical for our communities but also makes financial sense. As we move into post-COVID-19 recovery and define our "new normal," we have an opportunity to transform our care economy and provide sustainable solutions to recognize the importance of care work and to make quality care services accessible for all communities. It is an opportunity to debate and innovate ways to fix a broken system where solutions to date have not been wholesale, innovations have not accessed capital, and successful innovations have not been scaled. The old way does not work anymore, and there is money in fixing the system. The challenges outlined are primarily because most people who allocate capital lack proximity to the issues. Before 2020, they did not see the critical role that care work plays in sustaining economies and the opportunity it could present in overall economic growth.

Growing the economic pie through investing in care work requires deep interrogation of how to value care work and ensure that caregivers have the skills, salaries, and benefits needed for a good quality of life; engage men with the care economy and defy societal norms currently rein-forcing an unequal share of care work; create the pathways for economic independence for care workers (certification, entrepreneurship, leadership programs, career resources, financial literacy, and so on); and fund public investments in social infrastructure and enact regulations for better wages and working conditions.

With these steps, we can transition to a world in which care work is recognized as essential for the well-being and functioning of our societies and economies, redistribute unpaid care work and domestic responsibil-ities equally between men and women, and remunerate all care work. We need to develop solutions to improve access, affordability, and quality of care at all levels of the care ecosystem (early age care, eldercare, health-related care, disability-related care, and so forth). At the macro governmental level, we must enact better-informed care policies and offer care infrastructure financing. At the micro level, we must develop market-based approaches grounded in innovation and care entrepreneurship, and private sector companies must provide more robust employer-supported care benefits.

There are growing examples of innovations at the micro or private sector level, including one of the world's most well-known care economy companies called Care.com and some lesser-known companies such as Kido School. Care.com is an online marketplace for childcare, senior care, special needs care, housekeeping, and more. It raised $111 million before going public in 2014. It was acquired in 2020 and is no longer publicly traded.[359] Kido is an early-stage fran-chise platform designed to support the launch of thousands of micro early age schools. Because of technology, Kido can deliver curriculum and resources that support quality assurance, further strengthened by in-person random site visits. This strategy can enable entrepreneurial individuals to start neighborhood pods as instructors and grow into franchise owners as they can pay off start-up costs invested by the franchisor. Kido Village is the Indian platform that Kido is piloting to launch microschools across five major Indian cities.[360]

With the increasing need for eldercare, we are witnessing more innovation in this area such as the German-based start-up called Careship. Its model is robust because it is working on the talent supply chain, including professionalizing the space so that both male and female talent are attracted to the work.[361] There are many more examples of these types of private sector companies that will benefit from more investment capital allocation.

At the macro level, when governments fund care infrastructure and legislate care work benefits in a manner that signals its importance to the private sector and enables the market to appropriately recognize and value care work, private sector innovation will follow. The limited care infrastructure across most countries in the world, which includes disaggregated quality centers and no legislative requirements for private sector employers to provide adequate support and benefits to employees, is a major factor in the negative economic reality of women leaving the workforce during the worst of the COVID-19 pandemic. This phenomenon was occurring before the pandemic, but now the consequences of poor care economy infrastructure are starkly visible.

While the United States currently lacks public care funding, it is encouraging that the 2021 US infrastructure plan included unprecedented levels of funding support for the early age care economy ($200 billion for universal pre-kindergarten and childcare programs). Hopefully this plan will be enacted, but even if it is not, it signals newfound recognition of the critical role care work plays in a growing economy.[362] There is an opportunity to view this funding as similar to that which the US government put into seeding the development of technological breakthroughs that brought us companies such as Google.[363] If innovators can see this funding as a down payment on the necessary care economy infrastructure, they will start building businesses. If employers view it as a signal that the government will do their share in paying for some of these services, a significant market build-out will result. And if used as an example by other countries that lag behind the United States in childcare, this foundational investment will become a catalyst for a global investable universe with the potential to create an estimated 269 million jobs if investments in education, health, and social work doubled by 2030.[364] There are similar investment needs and opportunities in eldercare, especially in countries like Japan, which has a significant aging population.

Examples of successful innovations at the country-level demonstrate that wholesale change is possible. Norway's leadership in the care economy has its foundation in female leadership. In the 1970s, labor directives that favored men prompted women to march for their rights to equal employment, then equal rights in the workplace, followed by activism for regulations that created an enabling environment for their workforce participation.[365]

Since then, Norway has been researching, fine-tuning, and enacting policies that have allowed a robust public and private care economy infrastructure to grow with positive results. Today, the private sector provides 60% of care work, with government subsidies limited to centers that work within established government policy, including making sure services are affordable. There are three types of kindergartens in Norway on the public to private spectrum. Ordinary kindergartens can be public or private, offering half-day or full-day service year-round for children from birth to five years of age. Family kindergartens are based in private homes and have a maximum of five children supervised by a qualified teacher. Open kindergartens are part-time drop-in centers for parents and children to participate in activities. The hard infrastructure in these centers is of excellent quality. As the government program was ramping up and there were not enough spaces in centers, the government offered families money to cover wage losses if a parent had to stay home to care for their child. Data shows that this benefited parents across the economic spectrum, not just poor families.[366]

The government subsidizes centers with a generous legislated parental leave policy, about 70 weeks, which applies to both parents if they take it at separate times. This policy mandates that fathers must take an equal amount of leave to care for their children as mothers do. There is not enough data to say this will have a tangible effect on gendered care expectations down the road, but the policy itself is an impressive attempt to balance the care chasm between mothers and fathers. It will be interesting to study the long-term effects of this policy to see whether it does change the connection between gender and care work in Norway.[367]

Earlier, we asked the question of whether better pay and professionalization would lead to greater gender diversity in the sector. In some European countries, including Norway, gender diversity in the early age care centers has improved as the sector has required greater education levels, certifications, and offered better pay, benefits, and pension plans.[368]

Given the right incentive, the US private sector has provided the innovation and creativity to solve complex problems. There is potential to learn from different models in the world and unleash the power of ingenuity and capital markets for wholesale change. Imagine having the US government provide funding that can be used as seed capital to fund a Norwegian-style care system, customized for a US population that, at 333 million people, is 66 times that of Norway. Imagine the opportunity around the world as innovators in other countries customize local solutions, including in populous countries like India, where the model of small, home-based early age pods is in early experimentation. Coupling this with a central infrastructure to ensure quality, provide training, and even offer start-up and working capital raises significant potential for new businesses. There will be endless possibilities for innovation that will fuel economic growth.

A CARE ECONOMY INVESTING CHECKLIST

You are considering a seed investment in a start-up company that hopes to launch a disruptive innovation in the care economy space. What questions should you ask as part of your due diligence?

1. At the innovation stage, are women involved in the development of the solution? Are women on the design team?

2. Has market research been conducted that focuses on female users who currently represent most of the workforce? Have the findings been integrated into the solutions?

3. Has market research been conducted that focuses on potential male employees to understand what variables are key to attracting them into the sector? Have the findings been integrated?

4. Does the solution envision attracting both male and female talent and thereby offer attractive pay and benefits packages?

5. Does the solution target both physical (upgrading the physical spaces where caregiving happens) and human (offering training and certification programs) infrastructure?

HEALTH CARE

How will it look when all the principles of optimizing talent that we've discussed in this book—including fully utilizing female leadership and recruiting frontline health-care workers and collaborative leaders—are incorporated into a new US health-care system? This new system will optimize products and services to meet the needs of the primary health-care consumer (women) and lead to an overall integration of the health-care system that benefits everyone. Let's consider these changes and how investors can be prepared to take advantage of this new system.

The US health-care system is broken. The Commonwealth Fund benchmarked the 2015 performance of the United States compared to 10 other high-income countries and found the government, the private sector, and individuals in the United States spend more on health care than the other countries, yet our health outcomes are much worse. We have the lowest life expectancy and the highest incidence of chronic diseases.[369] These disappointing statistics are despite decades of talk about health-care reform, breathtaking health-care innovations, and passage of the Affordable Care Act. Current increases in health-care spending in the United States outpaces all other economic growth. The country's overall economy is being cannibalized by our health-care spending—and sadly, we don't even have positive health outcomes to show for it. If we want to grow the economic pie for everyone, restructuring the US health-care economy would be a wonderful place to start.

Currently, most of the health-care workforce in the United States and around the world is female, but the financial leadership across all stakeholders (hospitals, insurance companies, pharmaceutical companies, physician organizations) is predominantly male. As we've stated before, women make over 80% of health-care decisions in the United States, are more impacted by disease, and yet make up fewer than 31% of senior leadership positions in the broad health-care economy.[370] The dysfunctional health-care system will be fixed when women's leadership is applied to its institutions such as hospitals, insurance companies, and drug companies.

Let's consider three different aspects of US health care that will significantly improve when women participate in health-care innovation and financial leadership: (1) the macro system, (2) the micro system (or the individual interaction between consumers and the providers of care), and (3) the funding of innovation to develop new products.

At the macro level, the American health-care system depends on a fee-for-service model where physicians are reimbursed for the number of transactions they deliver rather than the health outcomes of their patients. A 2017 report indicated nearly 71% of medical reimbursement in the United States is still based on a fee-for-service model.[371] This model is flawed because the primary stakeholders in the system (hospitals, insurance companies, doctors, employers) have the incentive to deflect costs to one another rather than having aligned incentives to optimize the health of the patients and work together to decrease the overall costs in the system. Because the US health-care market places the most value on health-care transactions rather than actual health outcomes, the needs of the individual consumer (the patient) are deprioritized. For instance, in the case of patients with chronic knee pain, an insurance company pays a higher reimbursement for surgery than for physical therapy—even if the physical therapy is likely to result in less pain, less risk, quicker return to work for the patient, and less cost to the health-care system. In contrast to this fee-for-service model, there are some integrated systems within the United States (such as Kaiser Permanente or the Veterans Administration) that distribute shared incentives for health outcomes across physicians, hospitals, and insurance providers. In this type of integrated system, all stakeholders are financially rewarded if they keep patients healthier and minimize their use of services. There have been many legislative attempts in the United States to encourage health-care systems to become more integrated and collaborative (including capitation, medical homes, and the development of accountable care organizations); however, physicians still report that less than 50% of their revenue comes from some sort of values-based compensation or integrated system.[372]

Another example of the consequences of a disintegrated health-care system is in how abortions are provided in the United States. What should be a simple and low-cost service that's available throughout the health-care system or community has become very complicated and costly— largely due to social stigma and politics. Almost 25% of women will have an abortion in their lifetime, yet access in many states is remarkably limited.[373] This leads women to delay getting care and to take more time off work to drive longer distances—costing them, their families, their employers, and their states considerable expense. At the national level, the Institute for Women's Policy Research (IWPR) estimates that state-level abortion restrictions cost state economies $105 billion per year by reducing workforce participation and earnings levels while increasing turnover and time off from work among women aged 15 to 44 years.[374] In their report, IWPR identifies that states with the fewest abortion restrictions and the most integration of services are able to prevent this economic loss and better support their female workforce.

What will a new health-care system look like when women have larger roles in health-care innovation and financial leadership? Fundamentally, integrated health-care systems require collaborative leadership in making decisions to meet the needs of multiple stakeholders rather than a purely hierarchical decision paradigm. As we've described previously, women excel at collaborative leadership. Women will start by building a health-care economy that values outcomes instead of transactions. This type of system would match the supply of services to the demand and would take the best care of the consumer while providing cost efficiency for all the financial stakeholders. A diverse and collaborative leadership would address the needs of all communities and would be integrated in a manner that allows cost sharing, profit sharing, and prioritization of the best health outcomes for the patients. The supply of services that impact health (whether it's the workforce of social workers, dieticians, and therapists, or anger management programs for abusive spouses) would match the demands from the consumers. In specific regard to the provision of abortion services, we recognize that the social and political issues that impact access to abortion services in the United States are not going away anytime soon. However, when women have more control of the financial decision-making among all entities that are impacted by women's lack of access to abortion care—including government and corporate leadership—the system will work better for women who need abortions. The current inefficiencies and costs to governments and employers would decrease. A newly designed system like this will remove redundancy and inefficiency from the market. It will allow individuals to be more productive as employees, students, or caregivers.

On the micro level of a patient's individual interaction with doctors, we face a separate set of flaws. Currently in the United States, the most expensive providers are often the ones who see patients first in extremely high-cost "in-person" settings. Whether it's in an emergency room, community clinic, or private doctor's office, an expensively educated and relatively well-paid physician (or physician extender such as a nurse practitioner or physician's assistant) is often the first engagement a consumer (patient) has with the health-care system. These providers are usually the ones that dictate the treatment protocols and design the systems for care in what is often referred to as a "doctor-centric" model. Consumers must take time off from their normal obligations of work, school, or caregiving and come to a doctor's office, sit in a waiting room, and then do their best to communicate to the doctor all the complicated factors in their lives that might be influencing their health. The interrogation should include any childhood history of adverse experiences, the type of work they do, and any toxic environmental exposures as well as a discussion of family dysfunctions such as violence, mental illness, or alcoholism. Then there are all the important questions that address disease prevention, such as whether they exercise, eat a good diet, smoke, or use harmful drugs. This all must fit in the typical 15- to 30-minute appointment for most primary care physicians. In some cases, a patient has a consistent doctor who knows their history and already knows the answer to many of the questions, but in many cases a patient will meet a new doctor every time they access the health-care system. This doctor-centric system doesn't prioritize the needs of patients or their caregivers (who are most often women) and leads to waste, inefficiency, communication errors, and poor health outcomes.

Doctors who work in this system are at a disadvantage too. They have limited time to spend with their patients to get to know all the factors that influence their patients' health. They are not trained to consider all these influencers and don't have the tools to treat them properly. For instance, studies have shown that nonmedical factors (social and behavioral determinants) are the cause of 60 to 70% of health outcomes in the United States.[375] Despite considerable advancement in the understanding of the social determinants of health, doctors learn to focus on pharmacology and surgery as treatments rather than diet and lifestyle. A person's health may be harmed by conditions such as domestic violence or toxic stress, but doctors are rarely equipped to provide the appropriate treatments. All the latest pharmacological advancements or fancy laser laparoscopic techniques won't fix a patient who is suffering from the impact of violence in her home.

How will female financial leadership help fix the dysfunction at the micro level between patients and doctors? Because women are the primary consumers of health care, and the primary health-care workforce, they are closest to the challenges and thus best equipped to provide innovative solutions. A system that is redesigned to meet the needs of female consumers and a female workforce will look more like the following.

The "frontline" workers (i.e., the first providers that individuals encounter, whether for new problems, management of chronic problems, or for preventive care) will specialize in addressing behavioral and social situations.

They will often be social workers or health educators.[376] The first encounter with the health-care system will happen in the patient's home or workplace to allow a full assessment of the environment that contributes to the health outcome of that individual. A system that prioritized community-based social workers and health educators as the frontline caregivers will result in more effective and cost-efficient use of resources and care that is culturally aligned with individuals and their communities. Doctors will still have a significant role in this system, but only if the patient has a problem that requires medications or surgery. Societies that utilize community health workers have seen better preventive health outcomes and a decrease in long-term chronic diseases, fewer hospitalizations, and a decrease in overall health-care costs.[377] If the overall cost of providing care in the United States decreased, more capital would be available for innovation and allow broader growth of the US economy.

In addition to the macro and micro dysfunctions in the US medical system, there is a particular deficit in funding for innovation in women's health. As in other industries that we've described, the needs of female health-care consumers are not being addressed. As an example, let us consider the importance of contraception and maternal health and the inadequate funding for scientific development in these fields. The single most significant health decision confronted every day by women between the ages of 15 to 50, as well as their families, is whether they want to be pregnant. The decision to have children or prevent pregnancy has a cascade of financial ramifications because childbearing is the most significant disrupter of a woman's career trajectory. The availability of contraception is essential—not only for the health of an individual woman but for her family, community, and beyond, including her employer.

The health-care system (including insurance companies, employers, and the government) spends an enormous amount on contraception. Prescription contraception methods—including pills, injections, implants, and intrauterine devices (IUDs)—are one of the largest pharmaceutical categories. In 2018, the Guttmacher Institute estimated that in the United States there are 13.2 million birth control pill users, 1.4 million injections, 1.5 million implants, and 6.1 million IUD insertions.[378] The overall US contraceptive market has been estimated to be over $9 billion in 2021.[379] Despite this enormous expenditure, almost 50% of pregnancies in the United States are still unintended.[380]

In the case of maternal health, the cost to our system is also enormous. Depending on the location of the delivery, cesarean sections are among the top three most common surgical procedures in the United States, with 1,186,397 performed in 2018.[381] The cost of a cesarean section has been estimated to be $22,646, which would mean that the cost to the US economy of providing cesarean sections is at least $26 billion.[382] The overall societal cost of caring for both mothers and babies due to just one complication of pregnancy, preterm delivery, was estimated in 2005 to be $26.2 billion annually.[383] Despite this expenditure, the maternal death rate in the United States (especially for Black women) is astoundingly high, with 44 Black women dying for every 100,000 live births in 2019.[384] (This rate is four to five times higher than the rate for US white women and makes the United States the least-safe developed country in which to have a baby.[385]) Contraception and maternal health are two examples of where tremendous spending has failed to result in improved health outcomes, largely due to a lack of innovation.

There has been no significant innovation in contraceptive and maternal health technologies in the last 40 years. Since Ruth began her career in obstetrics and gynecology in 1986, contraception and support for women in childbirth has not changed. We are still using the same hormonal combinations that were invented in 1954 and the same fetal monitoring systems that were in use in the 1980s. The rates of poor maternal health outcomes have only gotten worse in this time. Simultaneously, in those same 40 years, there has been no significant increase in government or private sector allocation of capital for contraception or maternal health innovation. The natural market forces that would otherwise provide supply/demand/value solutions to these problems are constrained by lack of research prioritization and, as is the case with abortion, by social stigma and politics.

The funding for research and development of new contraceptive products and for improved maternal health care is only a fraction of money spent to develop new oncological therapies. The NIH reports that in 2020, $593 million was allocated for contraception/reproduction research, whereas $7 billion was for cancer—which doesn't include the $4.8 billion for research into specific types of cancer.[386] Yet enhancements in reproductive and maternal health technology could have a significantly higher impact on health, the cost of providing health care, and the productivity of our workforce than technology enhancements in oncology. And while in this discussion we are focusing on the US markets, any technological advancement in the United States would benefit the health outcomes in markets around the world.

When venture capital investment decisions in health-care technologies are made by female general partners, the populations that need innovation will be better represented and the current gaps in services will be better addressed. When Black women are making decisions about which new maternal health technologies are going to have the biggest impact on preventing Black maternal deaths, we will finally see an improvement in US maternal mortality. When research and development into new products and the entrepreneurs and founders of the early stage companies are being led by these same women who reflect both the health and financial needs of their communities, we will see a flow of capital to the development of new nonhormonal, highly effective, and reversible contraception; new platforms to provide abortion pills through the mail; and new alternative birth centers to allow people to give birth in environments that are culturally congruent for them. All these changes will result in a more stable workforce, improved productivity and employee retention, and more long-term financial gains for investors.

When women have more opportunity to direct finances in health care, there will be a pipeline of capital investments in modern technologies and treatments that also address the gaps in innovation that are likely to have the biggest impact on the health of the population, including treatment of issues such as toxic stress, gun violence, and smoking. There will be a better match between the development of innovative technologies and the systems that need to be fixed, resulting in a more robust flow of capital to fund these new products, happier consumers, and more money for the investors. This sort of system redesign will remove cost from the system, deliver to the consumer a more reliable product, and grow the economy.

Will women design a better health-care system for the US economy? Using collaborative leadership, they would ensure that all stakeholders shared the incentive to improve health outcomes utilizing integrated delivery models. Women are best equipped to design the delivery system that shifts from an inefficient and costly doctor-centric model to one that meets the health needs of all consumers. And given the lack of prioritization for funding of contraception and maternal health-care innovation, women would be able to redirect the flow of capital in these sectors.

If the capital that is perpetuating inefficiencies would be directed to growing the economy more broadly, we would all benefit. This would be particularly true if the investments addressed the problem of constrained markets and lack of capital for contraception, abortion, and maternal health. Women and their families will benefit if they have access to the best technologies to make informed decisions about when and how to have children. Scientists and entrepreneurs would have more financial support to develop these technologies. Employers and governments who pay most health-care costs for their workers will benefit from a healthier and more productive workforce. Ultimately, everyone benefits from a healthier workforce and economic growth, especially the smart investors who are prepared for these changes.

A Health-Care Investing Checklist

You are considering a Series A investment in a new company in the health-care space. How can you be sure the company is optimizing female decision-making strategies?

1. Are women in leadership positions in the company? This could be at the CEO, CFO, or COO level. Are there women founders and board members?

2. Do the other investors in the company include women fund managers or limited partners?

3. Does the company specifically analyze the market for female consumers? Have they engaged female focus groups?

4. Has the company specifically addressed the impact of their products or services on the health-care workforce? Have they engaged focus groups of frontline health-care workers?

5. Has the company considered the impact of its products or services on the overall health-care system? Is there potential for "collateral damage" or unforeseen consequences over the long term that need to be addressed?

6. How does the company treat its own workforce? Does it pay a living wage and consider benefits such as paid leave?

7. Is the company addressing existing inefficiencies in the health-care system that could contribute to better health outcomes, better experiences, and at less cost?

ENVIRONMENT

What will the world look like when women are fully part of the financial decision-making that impacts the environment? Would climate change be mitigated when women have financial leadership? Would the resulting impact on the environment lead to higher returns on investments and economic growth? The impact of women's leadership on climate will affect both the micro (community) and macro (national and government) levels. The impact will be a cleaner, more sustainable environment as well as economic growth and financial returns for investors because women are closer to the problems that result from climate change, including migration, food insecurity, loss of clean water, and disruption from extreme weather events. This proximity makes them better positioned to develop innovative solutions. Furthermore, more collaborative leaders with longer-term thinking are well suited for the collective long-term action that's needed to confront climate change.

At the micro or community level, women are often the most impacted by weather events and are often the source of creative solutions that take the long view into account. When women are in the financial decision-making circles that manage these local events, their firsthand knowledge of the problems contributes to solutions that not only include the needs of women in their communities but are beneficial for all. At the macro level, whether through the control of corporate strategies or as heads of state or CEOs, women are more likely to make financial decisions that contribute less to climate change and result in environmentally beneficial policies.[387] These environmentally beneficial changes from both micro- and macro-level activities result in significant economic growth.

As we've discussed in previous chapters, women are differentially impacted by climate change for many reasons. According to the United Nations, 80% of people displaced by climate change are women.[388] Because so many women serve as primary caregivers and providers of food, they are more likely to be affected when flooding and drought occur. When such disasters happen, they must travel farther and spend more time acquiring food and water for their families. Sources of clean drinking water are disappearing in many ways that harm women. Research following Hurricane Andrew in 1992 found immense discrepancies between the experiences of women and men in the aftermath of the storm. "Hurricane Andrew, Through Women's Eyes: Issues and Recommendations," a study done by anthropologists Betty Hearn Morrow and Elaine Enarson, found that "being female was an important dimension which appeared to increase the negative effects of being a victim and to retard personal and family recovery, especially when compounded with poverty and minority status."[389] Looking into the gendered dimension of hurricane relief, the researchers found women made up the majority of people seeking primary assistance. The same study argues that because of women's likelihood at bearing more of the brunt of a disaster, they should be much more involved at the policy level for future disaster relief planning.

Enarson and Morrow report on the feminist organizing that happened in Miami-Dade County community following Hurricane Andrew. An organization called We Will Rebuild was established with the aim of raising and distributing private funds for emergency relief. Participation in this effort was by invitation and included very few women or people of color.[390] Critics of this effort charged We Will Rebuild with "emotional distance and posturing when board members toured devastated areas in air-conditioned buses."[391] In response, a new organization called Women Will Rebuild was launched as a coalition of women's groups to reprioritize women's needs for funding. This organization was led with open, democratic meetings, and over fifty women's groups joined the coalition.[392] While the Women Will Rebuild coalition disbanded, it "influenced the board decision to fund teen pregnancy services and contribute over $2.1 million for childcare services. . . . with this increased female presence on the executive and finance committees, substantial funds were allocated to domestic violence programs and youth recreation services."[393] This is a fitting example of how including diverse women in solution-building improved outcomes for all.

Women are on the front lines of the battle to combat the impact of climate change. The nature of women's circumstances, including less access to human rights, frequently working agricultural jobs, and being more likely to live in poverty, makes them more vulnerable than men during climate-related disasters.[394] Climate disasters not only create new and unforeseen threats, such as "once in a lifetime" freezes, heat waves, and floods that now occur yearly, but also serve to exacerbate existing inequalities. If women are already primary caregivers, housekeepers, and food providers, the burden of nursing an injured or ill person back to health, recovering a home from a flood, or finding water for the household following a disaster will naturally befall them. In these cases, climate change exacerbates the unequal risks inherent in traditional gender roles.[395]

This increased risk rate for climate-related struggle makes women better suited than men to address and fight climate change because they know more intimately the challenges we are all facing. The scope of the problems requires a collaborative leadership model to generate solutions where individuals and grassroots organizations share stories and innovative solutions across communities and continents. Leaders across the globe then need to accept, fund, and implement these solutions.

In her book *Climate Justice: A Man-Made Problem with a Feminist Solution*, Mary Robinson offers many examples of what this type of leadership model should look like in action. Robinson was the president of Ireland from 1990 to 1997.[396] She resigned from the presidency two months before the end of her term to take on the role of United Nations High Commissioner for Human Rights. She continues to be a strong advocate for international human rights and climate justice. In her book, Robinson provides many examples of women who have been directly impacted by climate change because of the loss of jobs in the fossil fuel industry, instability of crops on their farms, and the devastation of their homes and communities from extreme weather. In these cases, women came together to form community-based organizations where they share their stories and solutions and then drive collective action.[397] She describes the story of Natalie Isaacs, an Australian woman who first committed to reduce her own consumption and then launched the 1 Million Women initiative to recruit other women from around the world to make the same commitment. This is a notable example of the multiplier effect that female consumers can have. It's particularly remarkable that Robinson, a former head of state and powerful world leader, personally joined the 1 Million Women organization. In her book she says, "Like... hundreds of thousands of 1 Million Women members, I learn as I go. But by undertaking the journey to reduce our carbon footprint, we participate in a global movement that has real capacity for change. When faced with the enormity of the climate change problem, it is easy to throw our hands up in the air and admit defeat. But individual empowerment leads to confidence."[398] As of this writing, 1 Million Women has 1,010,821 members who have pledged to reduce their collective carbon emissions by 704,728,717,445 tons in total.[399]

There are many other examples of women driving local innovation, attention to climate change, and collaborative leadership. For instance, in 2001 Raghab Chattopadhyay and Esther Duflo studied the impact of mandated local female leadership on the village councils in West Bengal. They found that women elected as leaders prioritized public projects that include access to clean drinking water, access to fuel, and road construction.[400] In other examples of the impact of local innovation, women make decisions that reduce food insecurity. If women farmers were given equal access to resources, they could boost total agricultural output in developing countries by 2.5 to 4%, thereby reducing the number of undernourished people in the world by 100–150 million (12 to 17%).[401] These types of local activities in which women participate in financial decision-making are critical to building healthier communities and stronger economies. And stronger economies will lead to more investments to prepare, protect, and support populations against climate disasters.

As food shortages are one of the most devastating consequences of climate change, it is essential that we optimize the world's food production. Gender imbalances in small-scale farming have rendered female farmers unable to achieve the same yield as their male counterparts. Even though women make up 43% of this industry, due to their relative lack of access to financial support and burden of domestic duties they produce on average 20 to 30% less than their male counterparts.[402] With a warming planet and a dwindling food supply, we cannot accept suboptimal food production for the sake of gender conformity. Leveling the farming field will not only empower female farmers but will have the practical benefit for all people of quite literally creating more pie (and other necessary food items).

On a larger scale, we see examples of women leaders tackling climate change across the globe. Ask any person to name a climate activist, and there is a strong chance that they name Greta Thunberg. Alongside Greta's star-power presence is the young Ugandan activist Vanessa Nakate, who is raising awareness of the continued burning of the Congo Basin, the world's second-largest rainforest and the "lungs of Africa."[403] There is also Tara Houska, a tribal lawyer of the Couchiching First Nation tribe, one of the leaders in the long, successful fight against the Keystone XL Pipeline. These are just three women leaders among countless other climate activists at the global and local scale.[404] All of these women rely on collaborative, highly networked leadership styles to generate social change to improve the environment and diminish the risks of climate change.

What about at the macroeconomic or systemic level? How will women's leadership in the environment sector produce higher financial returns for investors? The answer to this question can be seen in how women's influence over ESG investing has changed the investment landscape. In March 2021, Joan Michelson reported in *Forbes* that ESG is the most popular investment strategy, and it has financially outperformed other investment strategies. She says that while ESG was "previously considered a niche investing strategy ... [it] is now the star, and women are a key part of why."[405] Michelson reports that female investors are almost twice as likely as their male counterparts to prioritize ESG elements when deciding which companies to invest in. And as investors are reassured that they can make money with ESG strategies, there's been a significant shift of capital into these products.[406] According to the Forum for Sustainable and Responsible Investment (also known as US SIF), "As of year-end 2019, one out of every three dollars under professional management in the United States—$17.1 trillion—was managed according to sustainable investing strategies." This is up 42% from $12 trillion just two years prior.[407]

The report also addresses the financial returns of ESG investing, stating, "A number of studies have found that investors do not have to pay more to align their investments with their values, or to avoid companies with poor environmental, social, or governance practices. Studies with such findings have come from Oxford University, the Global Impact Investing Network, the Morgan Stanley Institute for Sustainable

Investing, Nuveen TIAA Investments, and Deutsche Asset & Wealth Management, among others."[408] Another study of ESG-focused mutual funds and ETFs conducted by the Morgan Stanley Institute for Sustainable Investing found that there is "no financial trade-off in the returns of sustainable funds compared to traditional funds, and they demonstrate lower downside risk."[409] Moreover, during a period of extreme volatility, the study found "strong statistical evidence that sustainable funds are more stable."[410]

While ESG investing is still being led by women (*Fortune* reported in 2020 that "over the past five years, 44% of the new recruits to top ESG jobs that Acre Resources helped fill went to women"), sustainable investing has broken through to the mainstream investment houses.[411] In his 2021 Letter to CEOs, BlackRock CEO Larry Fink wrote, "We know that climate risk is investment risk. But we also believe the climate transition presents a historic investment opportunity."[412]

What can we learn about the impact of women in leadership at companies and the performance of those companies on environmental issues? A recent report from the International Finance Corporation provides evidence that more women in business leadership positions promote higher environmental, social, and governance standards, particularly when women constitute a critical mass of 30% or more on company boards.[413] The Sasakawa Peace Foundation reported in 2020 that when boards have three or more active female members, their companies have more consistent climate-related disclosures and a better track record of developing policies and methods for addressing climate change.[414]

Women in nonclimate leadership roles include climate measures in their fields of expertise. We have seen that women do not wait until they have been invited to a climate summit; they implement climate measures wherever they are. Other studies show that 60% of women want to work for firms that care about sustainability compared to 38% of men, and "women are more likely to perceive global issues—such as pollution, conflict, and inequality—as 'very serious', to care about how and where products are made, to be more concerned about environmental problems, and to be classified as sustainably minded consumers."[415]

Clearly, women are leading the way implementing sustainable practices outside the traditional climate realm. Fighting climate change will require leadership from all sectors (not just farming and water-collecting), and ESG financial managers will need to look for climate solutions in all investments. Women are engaged in climate solutions in ways that men aren't—not necessarily because of some perceived innate understanding of the earth or sense of responsibility for our planet, but because a combination of their lived experiences and corporate values tends to make them focus on long-term sustainability rather than short-term gain. Women's insights along the whole spectrum of capital from farms to corporate CEOs to government policy-making tables will have an immensely positive effect on our fight against climate change.

So how does all of this relate to your investments, preparing for the next economy, and the value of women's financial leadership? Women are driving ESG investing, which is very profitable for the financial industry. In addition, there are benefits for the environment and growing the economy. The Smith School reported in 2020 that an increase in a firm's ESG performance in each country is associated with a statistically significant positive effect on living standards in that country, as measured by GDP per capita.[416] Environmental performance has a statistically significant positive effect for growth in per capita GDP in emerging economies. But ESG performance must be more than just commitments. Companies must follow through. Women's leadership at both the micro and macro level will be essential for the pivot of the financial markets to address climate change. And the resulting development of new investment vehicles, new renewable energy industries, and new job markets is making lots of money for investors and growing the economy.

AN ENVIRONMENT INVESTING CHECKLIST
How can you optimize female decision-making regarding the environment when considering an investment in a public company?

1. Are women in leadership positions in the company? This could be at the CEO, CFO, or COO levels and across other leadership ranks. Do women make up more than 30% of the board's membership?
2. Has the company been transparent about its environmental policies—within both its own operations and supply chain?
3. Will climate migration or food shortages affect the company's operations or workforce? How is it addressing this risk?

4. How does the company treat its own workforce? Are women promoted at the same rate as men? Does the company pay a living wage and consider benefits such as paid leave?
5. Does the company engage female focus groups to help shape its products and services?

Case Story: Intrinsic Exchange Group:
Driving a New Asset Class and Ensuring
Women Are at the Table

What if a new financial infrastructure offers investors the opportunity to assign value to nature's assets and prioritizes allocating capital to the solutions implemented by those closest to the challenges? According to Project Drawdown, 24% of greenhouse gas emissions come from agriculture and forestry activities.[417] And Project Drawdown's list of top three solutions (eliminate food waste from farm to table and reimagine diets, protect the land, and use farming processes that limit the escape of methane into air) to mitigate these emissions presents an example of why women must be in the rooms developing solutions. Women are key players in demand-side climate mitigation as well as essential stakeholders in global farming. It is not surprising that the debut of a trading platform to trade companies designed to protect the value of nature, under a partnership between the Intrinsic Exchange Group (IEG) and the New York Stock Exchange (NYSE), was of interest to Women of the World Endowment (WoWE). The vision is for Natural Asset Companies (NACs) to raise funds to promote conservation—in particular, agricultural practices—to protect the natural ecosystem. Currently, the economic system puts a value only on the output of land, such as products that come from agriculture and mining.

Following is an extract from a Changemakers Series conversation Patience had with Douglas Eger, CEO of IEG, discussing the development of this new asset class and women's roles.[418] Douglas is a veteran business leader, investor, and conservationist who sees NACs as a key to unlocking environmental health.

Patience: Could you walk us through what this process looks like? And who stands to benefit from a natural asset company?

Douglas: We announced a partnership (in 2021) with the New York Stock Exchange to be able to list Natural Asset Companies. This is a new asset class based on nature and its values. It is a special listing section, so these new forms of companies and the new asset class would have its own rules and the ability to structure a financial instrument in a corporate form that maps the value of nature. In this way we can work toward including natural capital—and to a large extent all human and social capital—within the mainstream of the economy.

Food companies are a great example. They would very much like to change their practices. I think they realize that a lot of industrial agriculture is extractive, it's not sustainable, and it's very damaging to biodiversity around the world, and yet, they're constrained . . . there's a limit to how much they can raise prices for goods and services.

Under the current regime, farmers are paid for the production of commodity crops, but they're not paid for creating room for wildlife or farming in a natural way. It should be that farmers and the supply chain in general are rewarded for being good stewards of the land as well as for producing a healthy food product. IEG fills the gap because there are investors who want to invest in protecting natural assets.

Patience: This is an incredible idea, that people can be compensated for saving the planet. Could you give us an example of how this will work?

Douglas: A concrete example of a client we have right now is a major consumer packaged goods company. They came to us and they said, "You know, we'd like to change our entire milk shed value chain." They're in the dairy business, and yogurt is a primary product line. They want to move from an industrial production to a regenerative one where, rather than cows being in barns and fed grain, they would be out grazing. That would have a tremendous impact on the landscape.

The way it works is farmers that are involved in the production would roll the natural capital values into a natural asset company, so they become major shareholders. The company would also be owned in part by the large food company that wants to make this investment.

When the NAC is formed, its value is based on the natural capital as well as some of the commodity output pricing. As an intermediate company, IEG could take the NAC public. The money from the IPO would be used to change the practices on the farm and to reconfigure the supply chain for the company.

Farmers then have the incentive to change their practices in line with growing natural capital because that's how the equity will be priced.

Patience: This is a strategy that's not just specific to farming.

Douglas: No, but several things happen in agriculture. It's important to think about how half the world's land surface is dedicated to agriculture. If we're going to deal with climate change, we're going to have to get that carbon back in the soil through these regenerative practices. It's one of our best, most cost-effective, and efficient ways to deal with climate change because half the planet's surface has been altered for agricultural use.

Patience: As we look around the world, and we look at how many women have title to land, the numbers are dismal. For instance, in Pakistan, 2% of the land is owned by women; in India, it's 13%. In Australia, I think it's 26%; in New Zealand, 20%. Women in places such as Africa are the majority of smallholder farmers, so they're farming the land, but they don't own the land. And yet, they're already producing value for communities. How do NACs include the idea of women as solution drivers, not just beneficiaries?

Douglas: We're licensing the rights to nature's production of ecosystem services and the intrinsic value of nature, not in a consumptive way, not a land ownership way. So that gives us flexibility. So for private lands, it's possible to map out the stakeholders. This is a public good for the world, and part of the prescriptions that we've been putting together with our rules at the exchange level; the charter of the company is broad benefit sharing.

Patience: And so there is potential for women to be involved in the ownership of these NACs, or we can have good gender equity in the leadership of these companies.

Douglas: Absolutely. You said something that really resonated with me, and that's women actors versus beneficiaries, and I think it's imperative that we build that into the DNA of the NACs. I look forward to working with you and others to draft additional best practices that would include these concepts as we're building rule sets. We are asking ourselves, what does it mean to be a natural asset company? What things must you do in order to be listed as a natural asset company? And these are exactly the types of issues that we should include. We should think of the broader scope of nature that if we don't have a society that is much more resilient and fairer, there will be no way to solve other problems that require us to pull together. If we're leaving a significant part of our human capital off the table, meaning women, we're not progressing very far.

WEALTH MANAGEMENT

Risk awareness, long-term perspectives, and collaborative management will be better leveraged when women control or manage more wealth. When we review the literature of the value chain of financial management, from households to investment committees, we see these traits exhibited repeatedly. When more women are in control of financial markets and public- and private-entity budgets, they utilize the traits they typically use to budget and spend money at the household level. The markets will benefit from the same spending and saving priorities of many women-run households. Skeptics will argue that lessons learned at the household level do not translate to the larger financial markets. However, we argue that the female tendency to save, invest, spend, and budget more efficiently and thoughtfully will translate to better stewardship of investment capital and the overall economy.

Although we have all witnessed in one way or another the trope of the "frivolous female spender," this image is a fallacy. From depictions in the media of women who cure their ills by shopping, to magazine stories directed at women about how to spend less, popular media is inundated with the idea that women overspend and over shop. Approximately 65% of money management articles in magazines represent women as excessive spenders.[419] Men and women tend to spend different amounts on different items. When it comes to depreciating purchases, women spend more on clothing items, but men spend more on cars. In contrast to the articles directed at women, 70% of articles written for men point to how making money is a masculine virtue to aspire toward.[420] Articles on investing also skew toward men as the target audience—a trend that is beginning to shift.

Contrary to these representations, the truth is that women budget and allocate household spending to the areas they are mostly responsible for or proximate to managing, such as nutrition, long-term health, and education spending for the whole family. Women also allocate their money to savings informed by a keener awareness of risks. This means that overall, less money is spent on items that build status and boost ego and more is put away for rainy days. For example, female microfinance borrowers spend more than 80% of their earnings and borrowings on their families' needs.[421] Recent studies show that gender differences in sensibilities regarding spending and saving cut across marital status and generations. A study by the Bureau of

Labor Statistics found that, in general, single women were more judicious in their spending than single men, spending less on food and alcohol—$3,680 and $234 per year, respectively, compared to $4,173 and $537 for single men. They are also more frugal in the prices they pay for goods and services, with 71% of women surveyed indicating that the last item they purchased was on sale, compared to 57% for men. Further, 74% of millennial women look for coupons for purchases compared to 65% of millennial men.[422] What would happen if more money were put into the hands of women by closing the gender pay gap? We will have more resilient households in the future, requiring fewer social safety nets and thereby creating the opportunity to direct fiscal budgets to invest in economic growth.

Savings behavior also differs by gender. Women save more of the lower earnings they make, informed by an acute sense of risk and the need to mitigate such risks, as discussed earlier. Reports consistently show women save a higher percentage of their paychecks at every salary level. A 2015 Vanguard study found that women are more likely to participate in workplace retirement plans, with more of their paycheck going to savings, and "across all income levels, women save at rates that are between 7% and 16% higher than men's savings rates."[423] According to a 2017 Fidelity report, women saved an annual average of 9% of their paychecks compared to an average of 8.6% saved by their male counterparts.[424] This trend is not new, so we should expect women to have more money saved. But, unfortunately, despite saving a higher percentage of their income, women still have less money saved relative to male peers at all stages, but especially later in life, due to the gender pay gap. On average, women make 82 cents versus each dollar a man makes.[425] A BlackRock survey published by CNBC highlighted data showing American women nearing retirement age having on average $81,300 in retirement funds, compared to male counterparts at $118,400.[426]

When women make as much money as their male peers for similar employment roles, there will be positive impacts on household spending budgets, as women would direct more money to nutritional needs and the health and wealth of their families. We will have healthier families and fewer households in poverty. Women would also retire with more savings, mitigating the burden on tax-funded social safety nets and freeing up tax dollars for other needs, like infrastructure, thus enabling overall economic growth.

This is certainly the case in Australia, where a national crisis caused by elderly women living longer than men and finding themselves destitute late in life was raising significant concerns. Australia was fortunate that one of the first female employees at the bank now known as Westpac pushed to be included in its retirement fund, which was, at the time, offered only to its male employees. Beatrice Tennyson Miller worked for Westpac for 41 years, during which time she repeatedly advocated for women's inclusion in the bank's retirement fund. She retired in 1938, one year after the bank finally included women in its retirement saving plan or superannuation fund.[427] For the next eight decades the superannuation offering was the same for men and women. Still, the problem of lower saved capital persisted for older women. To address the problem of more women finding themselves poor and destitute late in life, financial institutions developed additional superannuation products specifically targeted at women. These products offered the ability to purchase term-lengthening options that kick in after employer-provided retirement funds were depleted—a situation more women found themselves in not because they are poor savers but because on average they outlive men and make 82 cents for every dollar a man makes for comparable work. As a result, the private sector had the opportunity to innovate and grow their market share, and significant savings accrued to the national budget. Because Ms. Miller and other women advocated for change, it was easier to implement a private-sector solution that provided more robust social safety nets.

For Ms. Miller's generation, the challenge for women was to receive the same benefits as their male colleagues. The challenge for our generation is the closing of the gender pay gap. According to the Vanguard and Fidelity reports cited earlier, equal pay for women would put more money into their hands and would result in greater retirement savings. Similarly, workplace savings instruments such as IRAs and brokerage accounts also showed that, in proportion to their wages, women saved more. Women added an average of 12.4% annually to their account balance, compared to 11.6% for men.[428] Greater retirement savings will mean better outcomes for the health and wealth of families, freeing up room in national budgets, currently directed to safety nets, to invest in economic growth. The other thing to note is that these savings contribute to pension funds, which enlarges the capital pools that in turn invest for economic growth.

Motivations for savings differ along gender lines. A survey asking about the savings goals of millennials found that women save so they have the capacity to pay down debt, while men named saving toward a vacation as a priority, followed by debt repayment. Another form of savings is investing one's money, and men do a much better job of directing their earnings toward investing, making their money work for them. A BlackRock survey found that 70% of millennial men enjoy managing their investments, compared to 36% of millennial women.[429] We wonder if this lack of enjoyment is because women tend to want to know more before they take risks, and investing by its nature is risky, and whether the fact that they have less money to start with and tend to be more risk-aware lead to less appetite for allocating money into investments. Would closing the pay gap allow women to be less constrained in their investing strategies and to dedicate more money toward investing? When women earn more money, they will invest a greater share of it.

My (Patience) experience as an angel investor supports this trend. Earlier, we discussed how the percentage of angel investors in the United States who are women grew from 5% in 2004 to almost 30% in 2020.[430] As women have built wealth, they have embraced investing in the riskiest of asset classes: early stage investing. If we put more earnings in their hands, they would invest more in early stage companies that are solving the challenges we have described in the preceding sections. These investments would focus on the long term, beating back the challenges of climate change, the care economy, and health care. The health and wealth of individuals would improve, and economies would grow.

If women allocated more investment capital, we would see strong financial returns across all asset classes. Women would allocate more capital to innovations that benefit everyone, into risk-appropriate investments, and toward innovations that offer stable returns, resulting in more sustained gains for individuals and economies. History shows us that the characteristically female traits that inform women's management and investment behavior would be consistent across all environments. We can assume that larger pools of capital would also benefit from steady, well-considered strategies with better risk management so that the upside would be more consistent over time. A 2018 report published by PIMCO titled "Women, Investing, and the Pursuit of Wealth-Life Balance" supports these assumptions.[431] When measuring the success of their personal portfolios, only 34% of women surveyed indicated that outperformance was important to them, with 61% citing steady income gains.

Relative female and male spending behaviors show women exhibiting the traits that we have discussed throughout our writing—including empathy and consideration for the whole family unit and long-term view of health and education. Similarly, savings behavior of putting away more of what they earn but doing so in a less risky manner is in line with the traits we discussed around how women tend to take more of a risk-aware approach. One of the conclusions from a 2018 Australian report titled "Using Survey and Banking Data to Measure Financial Wellbeing" is that people who lean toward living within their means, seek to be more knowledgeable about financial matters, and have regular savings habits are likely to have better financial well-being.[432] More financial well-being at the individual level translates to tailwinds for economies.[433]

We have discussed how women spend their money with greater planning, expend a larger share of their earnings on their families' well-being, and save a larger portion of their earnings to mitigate against future risks. Now we will ask the next natural question: what if women, who are better at managing personal and household budgets, had greater control over the budgets of small and large public and private entities? If women can allocate such budgets in ways that address the mitigation of critical pressing challenges experienced by their communities, would they show the same traits that can lead to the growth of the economic pie?

At the macro level, evidence from women's participation in governance tells us that the answer is *yes*. One example of the influence of women on government spending is in Timor-Leste (East Timor) where, by 2011, women made up 32% of parliament. Some of these women were authors of the government's Gender Responsive Budgeting program, initiated in 2008 when a decision was made to integrate gender perspectives into the performance indicators informing budget allocations. By 2011, budgeting included greater allocations to health, education, agriculture, commerce, industry, justice, and social solidarity, which led to more stable and positive results for the country's citizens.[434]

There are also studies from the Colombian city of Medellín, which started its smart-city initiative in the mid-1990s, experimenting with diffused and collaborative input from all levels of the community. This initiative hinged on including women's voices into many aspects of the city's governance, including the budgeting process, combating violence and crime, and using women's insights to implement an innovative approach to urban planning and social innovations. This city of two million had been a leading center for crime driven by drug trading. By 2019, partly due to the fall of the drug cartel and collaborative citizen participation in governance, crime levels had fallen to one-twentieth of what they had been in 1993, and two-thirds of the population had climbed out of poverty, with almost all citizens having access to free education, health care, and transportation.[435] Existing women's organizations that had been formed to combat gender-based violence and other social ills came together to support and vote for more female delegates to represent them in the city's diffused government structure. Women participated in high numbers, and in the 2012 local elections, 54.8% of 5,472 delegates elected were women. Most wanted to be delegates to the participatory budgeting process, as this was the entity within the city's participatory democracy apparatus that had the most power. Medellín's constitution required that part of the budget be allocated by citizens.[436] These women understood the power of participating in proposing and allocating budgets to innovative solutions to the city's many identified challenges. Their influence on these allocations has partly underpinned the positive results on the lives of Medellín's citizens and the city's economy.[437]

Given that women tend to be more disciplined savers, hold investments for longer by being less impulsive investors, generate more consistent and better returns over time, and are more disciplined spenders and budget allocators, why is it that too many people consider women to be less confident with financial matters? Returning to the point made in the earlier part of this section, mainstream capital markets' information channels play a role. If these positive outcomes were lauded in more channels read and viewed by men who control the larger part of asset pools, they would want more female talent in the rooms of budget and capital allocation. As with the Medellín example, when there is broader participation and leadership from women, there will be better and more sustained positive outcomes for all citizens.

It turns out that in capital markets, as in most things in life, the less overconfident study the market more and make better, more deliberate decisions. Because women are not overconfident about their ability to invest, they tend to do it well. In 2017, Fidelity reported that their women's portfolios performed better than men's by 0.4%, which may not seem like much but when compounded over time can make a significant difference in portfolio performance.[438]

Like most positive things about the female traits we have highlighted in this book and the positive outcomes we have detailed, investment-related observations are not new: reports on women's tendency to do better than men at investing dates back to the early 1990s. A study by the University of California–Berkeley, based on 35,000 brokerage accounts over a six-year period from February 1991 to January 1997, found that women generated returns that were 1% higher, on average, than men.[439] The good news is that we are reading more of this in the channels male asset owners and money managers generally turn to for information. According to a 2021 report by Goldman Sachs, professional female investors tend to do better than men—43% of women-managed mutual funds outperformed their benchmark in 2020, compared to just 41%

of those managed by men.[440] Better performance is partly informed by the fact that they research their allocations more deeply and stay with their choices for longer periods, riding through periods of high volatility. A Vanguard study found that women trade 40% less frequently than men.[441] And that, too, is not a recent trend. The Berkeley study also found that men traded 45% more than women in the six-year period. The extra trading reduced men's net returns by 2.65% a year, as opposed to 1.72% for women.[442]

What if the saving, investing, spending, and budgeting patterns that have proven over time to produce stronger performance became integrated into a model of what "good" capital investment looks like? Such a model would recognize that there is cognitive bias and missed opportunities when relying on certain ways of thinking—for example, the experiences of an investment committee made up of people with homogenous backgrounds and lived experiences, or of a process that discourages creativity and creative input. Women who invest tend to conduct deeper research, seek input from collaborators, and review the importance of an investment beyond its short-term financial outperformance. And they review the long-term strategic importance of an investment as part of likely strong long-term financial performance.[443]

It is clear that we all win when women manage bigger budgets and allocate more capital. As the 2019 report by FCLTGlobal observed, "The research is piling up. Companies that aim for long-term success tend to find it, while those who reach for short-term gains end up with lower corporate profits, reduced shareholder returns, and more limited job creation."[444] What the report neglected to say, but what we have demonstrated here, is that a shift to this more successful model would be fast-tracked with more women in decision-making and capital-allocation roles.

A WEALTH MANAGEMENT CHECKLIST

How can I optimize female financial decision-making for my personal investments?

1. Who is managing your money?
2. Is the investment committee at the firm managing your money diverse?
3. How are they allocating your money?
4. How is a gender analysis applied to your portfolio?
5. If the investment team is not diverse, can you have them benchmark their performance against a team that is diverse?
6. Does the research team that is making recommendations for investments include at least 30% women?

Case Story: Government Pension Investment Fund (GPIF): Catalyzing System Change Through Capital Markets

Investors of all sizes are watching Japan's Government Pension Investment Fund (GPIF) put its weight firmly behind environmental, social, and governance (ESG) investing, including a focus on gender. The single-largest pension fund in the world, overseeing $1.7 trillion in assets, has drawn a clear line in the sand for investing with a gender focus and is affecting systems change by wielding their capital to improve impact and performance.[445]

Former chief investment officer Hiro Mizuno, who is now United Nations Special Envoy on Innovative Finance and Sustainable Investments, spoke at a GenderSmart Investing Conference in February 2021, where he shared that "gender diversity is one of the most challenging, but in my opinion, the most promising agendas for GPIF to accelerate change, make society better, and . . . make good investments."[446]

In 2015 GPIF took its first steps into sustainable investing by signing the Principles for Responsible Investing (PRI) and publishing its own principles. Two years later, the organization began allocating funds to ESG investments, with an initial US$27 billion allocated to companies with good ESG scores and into three Japanese equities ESG indices, including the FTSE Blossom Japan Index and the MSCI Japan Empowering Women Index (WIN).[447]

In December 2020, GPIF signaled the fund will continue to incorporate ESG principles into its mammoth portfolio while prioritizing greater gender diversity. It expanded its investment to its global equity portfolios by investing $12.5 billion into two ESG benchmarks, allocating $9.7 billion to MSCI's ACWI ESG Universal Index and $2.9 billion to Morningstar's Gender Diversity Index.[448]

Large financial actors are not known for making massive changes or being first movers into unfamiliar territory. Yet that is what Hiro Mizuno and GPIF did. As Mizuno said,

> "Conventionally, asset managers are evaluated on their ability to create a portfolio that performs better than the rest of the market. When I found myself responsible for managing GPIF's $1.5 T fund and knowing that we are required to achieve 30-year sustainable performance—I concluded that

we won't be able to create a portfolio that is totally insulated from what's happening to society. Rather, we have to find a way to make the whole system more sustainable, which results in more sustainable performance."[449]

His challenge? How to align GPIF's professional responsibility to provide better financial performance and pursue something they believed would better impact society and financial systems. GPIF took a systems approach and shifted their mindsets and perceptions to look outside their discrete portfolios. The biggest innovation that they made was to recognize that the whole capital markets system needs to be better for GPIF to have better portfolio performance. They stepped away from focusing on the immediate performance of the portfolio and toward managing a holistic, long-term agenda for their portfolio, such as gender diversity.[450] The philosophy behind these investment decisions led to a "universal ownership" approach where they classified themselves as a systems owner charged with making sure that every single investment decision, whether it was internal or appointing external money managers, ensured that they aimed to minimize negative externalities.[451]

GPIF requested their fund managers list financially material ESG factors and announced that they would be held accountable for their own choices. Gender diversity was included in most of their lists. However, it became clear that the depth of gender diversity decision-making was too superficial and there was little structure to truly evaluate the strategies and their impact. In Hiro's words, "We needed to find out how to affect the system. We came up with the idea of using the gender lens index to push the idea forward and we also used the ESG matrix to evaluate external managers in how they incorporate gender diversity into their decision making."[452]

While everyone at GPIF agreed that gender diversity was important to their long-term performance, it was not easy to determine a path forward. Perspective shift was the start, but every time gender diversity strategies were discussed, the managers came out of the room saying, "It's going to be difficult." In Hiro's words,

> "It's not easy to create a consensus in our industry on something that positively affects performance; it's much easier to create consensus about something that is a potential risk. So I flipped the question. Let's stop discussing whether gender diversity is a positive attribute to our performance. Let's agree if a company fails to have gender diversity it is carrying inherent risk. Then it was much easier to get support. Risk is a very strong driver of behavior and performance for investment professionals."[453]

Early in 2016, the fund set up a new stewardship and ESG group under Hiroshi Komori, senior director of the Public Market Investment Department. The GPIF says the aim of the division was to strengthen the fund's fiduciary duty for beneficiaries by furthering stewardship and ESG activities from a more strategic perspective and to increase the understanding of responsible investment principles in Japan.[454] By the end of 2020, GPIF had almost $3 billion invested with a gender focus, quite possibly the largest known allocation by a single asset owner to gender investing.[455]

A pool of assets the size of GPIF's has the power to signal and drive standards in the markets in which it operates. GPIF monitors managers' fund performances both on portfolio construction and engagement. The organization also joined boardroom diversity initiatives, including the 30% Club in the United Kingdom and the Thirty Percent Coalition in the United States, which campaign for 30% representation of women on boards, in 2016.[456]

GPIF's commitment to sustainable and gender-focused investing is a clear message for companies to step up their game and for investors who care about increasing share price as well as effecting a more inclusive and robust economy. More importantly, it is creating a model for other asset owners to follow, changing the behavior not just of investors but of the financial industry.

CHAPTER 6

A CALL TO
ACTION

EIGHT IMPERATIVES
FOR A WINNING
PORTFOLIO

Women's influence over financial decision making regarding all types of capital allocation improves both health and wealth for everyone. How can an investor take advantage of this fact? You can do eight things to start on the right path: invest through women, hire more women, mentor more women, promote more women, design for women, vote for women, listen to more women, and, finally, tell your friends all about it! Though we are writing this call to action specifically for investors who are yet to consider or are looking into leveraging women's leadership, specifically financial decision-making leadership, this advice applies to everyone who is hoping to promote diversity and inclusivity to optimize talent for the next economy.

INVEST THROUGH WOMEN

When you are making decisions about how and who will be allocating money, do so through women or through teams or investment committees that include women. They are out there, but you must be intentional about finding them. Networks of women portfolio and fund managers, such as 100 Women in Finance or VC Include, are good places to start.

Since women like to do their research, make measured selections, and prefer to stay the course once they have constructed a portfolio, history suggests you will be pleased with the overall results of your portfolio over time. If you are investing venture capital, providing more funding to early stage ventures founded by women will provide more upside for each dollar disbursed, as women-run companies tend to be more capital efficient.[457] And the old excuse that a pipeline is tough to identify is no longer relevant. You can connect with incubators and accelerators that support female entrepreneurs to increase access to early stage opportunities. You can also co-invest with women-led venture funds, which are slowly growing in numbers—their pipelines tend to have significant numbers of women founders. If you are an investment advisor, consider prioritizing and recommending funds that have at least one woman as a general partner.

If you are making commercial loans to entrepreneurs or offering mortgages to new homeowners, you will have more reliable payback of those loans if you prioritize women as borrowers.[458] (And, because on average these portfolios have lower defaults, you should be offering better interest rates.)

If you are investing in a pharmaceutical or consumer product company that's considering its next acquisition, look for strategies that prioritize acquiring smaller companies being led by women. You will find well-developed R&D with real market relevance, closing gaps that women scientists are keen to close because in many cases they address women's health issues, which have traditionally been underfunded.

And while we don't traditionally think of consumers as investors, you are technically investing in companies when you make purchasing decisions. As a consumer, find out where the women-led shops and services are in your neighborhood. Chances are, you'll be very satisfied with their products and the service you will receive. Additionally, you'll know that by supporting a woman-led small business, you are more likely to be supporting her family and community. It is easy to find them, too, with a simple Google

Maps search of "women-led shops near me." Women will be excellent stewards of your assets—whether it's as your investment advisor, manager of a mutual fund, the CEO of a company you've invested in, or the purveyor of the consumer goods you purchase.

HIRE MORE WOMEN

Not so long ago, conversations about hiring more women tended to conclude with, "We cannot find them for the roles we are looking to fill," especially in STEM-related fields. That cannot be the response anymore. Universities are admitting and graduating more women in all areas, including historically male-dominated ones.[459] Men have always had networks and women have recognized their importance and are creating powerful networks such as Women Who Code, Girls Who Invest, and 100 Women in Finance, which make for concentrated pools of excellent talent. Leverage women's networks to reach out directly to women.

Whether you are an investment advisor, bank, or a Fortune 500 company, organizations can find the talented women they need, and they can and should hire more than one to create a critical mass of allies and role models, thereby enhancing the potential that each of the women will succeed and the organization will benefit.[460] Companies will enjoy more upside from building a decision-making infrastructure with characteristics of collaboration, differentiated thinking, better risk awareness and stewardship of resources, and longer-term views, thereby ensuring more sustained resilience and profitability.

What will it take for your organization to succeed in bringing in strong female talent? It starts with intentionality, in the same way that you would develop a strategy for winning a client who would bring positive results to the bottom line. Be thoughtful from the start of the process, including making job postings more inclusive by removing language that alienates female applicants and by including women's photos in recruiting collateral—and not just photoshopped images. Goldman Sachs, for example, promotes both women employees and initiatives on the "Life" section of its LinkedIn company page as well as its careers blog.[461] Be aware of what types of environment will attract women and work to create it. According to the Wharton School study Four for Women, a company is good for women when it employs a significant percentage of women at every level and in every unit, pays equally for equal work, supports and protects the health of employees, and provides good working conditions.[462]

Companies that recognize the realities of most women's lives in and out of the office do better in recruiting them. Women tend to be the main caregivers in their families, so they are more attracted to jobs that promote flexible work, working from home, and additional medical benefits.[463] Women need to know that the jobs they are applying for will allow them to take time off when necessary and will not punish them for starting or caring for a family. They need to know that, even when their careers are not linear like those of most male employees, there will be room for career development.

A 2020 Glenmede report included an original analysis of data from Equileap that found companies in the top quintile of pay equity, access to benefits, training, and career development demonstrated greater returns and lower risk than companies in the bottom quintile of these features.[464]

Companies that recognize that women do not thrive in "boys will be boys" work environments win female talent. From emergency medicine to office jobs, women usually do not apply to jobs that promote a machismo working environment. Traditionally male-dominated fields looking to bring on female talent need to ensure their recruitment postings do not include language that heavily focuses on individual accomplishments. In line with how women operate, it is important to use words such as *teamwork* and *collaboration* instead. These indicate an empathetic work environment that enables employees to deliver greater value. The recruitment process should include diverse staff, including women from junior to senior levels, who can demonstrate they are thriving. Women want to work at organizations where they see other women succeeding.[465]

MENTOR MORE WOMEN

As anyone who has had a successful career will tell you, having good mentors is essential. As an investor, look for companies that have successful mentor programs. An effective mentor is a coach, advocate, problem-solver, networker, and barrier buster. It's not unusual for strong mentorship bonds in the workplace to develop among people of the same identity. Often men mentor men and women mentor women. But, especially in industries where female leadership is scarce, men need to step up as allies and mentors to optimize women's talent.

A 2014 EY report titled "Shaping the Future Together: Male Champions for Gender Equity: Experiences, Drivers and Lessons Learned" concluded that "strong and committed sponsorship plays a crucial role, as illustrated by numerous critical incidents where male champions stood up for female proteges in performance reviews and promotion rounds; ensured they were considered for career opportunities; increased their visibility within the organization; [and] helped expand their networks by introducing them to important stakeholders."[466]

The study goes on to say that good mentorship includes overcoming biases and stereotypes. A good mentor coaches the mentee about significant career moves or advancement, either within the company or externally. This can be difficult and feel awkward when the two parties in the relationship come from divergent backgrounds or have quite different barriers to success. Therefore, the most essential elements in a good mentor relationship are building trust, asking open-ended questions, and fully understanding the issues and challenges that the mentee faces every day.

Another crucial element of good mentorship is the willingness to be outwardly enthusiastic about the talents and capabilities of the mentee. As David Smith and Brad Johnson indicate in their book *Good Guys: How Men Can Be Better Allies for Women in the Workplace*, a man who is mentoring a woman needs to be comfortable with "sponsoring women loudly" because "talented women don't get enough of it."[467] Authentic, sincere praise and demonstration of respect for the abilities of women in the workplace are extremely powerful and culture-changing.

Good mentors use their social capital to open doors for mentees—this can mean making introductions, inviting her to join meetings, or putting in a good word when she is considering a new career move. A good mentor within an organization will recommend their mentee for "stretch" opportunities. This is often necessary because women tend to be socialized not to volunteer in the workplace and to be more reluctant to be their own champion. Women often assume their own performance will be noticed and result in promotion. With a good internal mentor, a woman's talent can be recognized and rewarded. And, also very importantly, as mentees reach positions of leadership within organizations, it's essential to continue to "telegraph your support . . . serve as an honest consultant, sounding board, and loyal follower."[468]

PROMOTE MORE WOMEN

As an investor, look for companies that do a fantastic job not only of recruiting and retaining women but also promoting them. Promoting more women starts with being intentional about having more women at all levels, across every unit of the company—one of the four characteristics of companies that are good for women as cited in the Wharton report.[469] This starts with acknowledging the inadequacy of the traditional response companies give when asked why they promote so few women to senior levels, such as, "We let our employees know when positions are available, but fewer women apply."

It is the responsibility of companies to create career advancement pathways to success that are equally appealing to men and women. Women are less likely to put themselves up for promotions for several reasons, including the fact that the numbers of other women or allies dwindle the higher one goes. Companies need to facilitate inclusive paths upward, including creating manageable workplaces, so women do not feel the need to sacrifice a promotion for their family life or vice versa.

In fact, if companies want qualified and capable talent at every level, they should promote the female talent already working for the company. As observed in the research by Joyce Ehrlinger and David Dunning, compared to men, women consider themselves less ready for promotions for which they are overqualified.[470] Men, on the other hand, are likely to overestimate their abilities. This means when a man enters a new role, the company often pays for him to get up to speed and takes on the greater risk of underprepared leadership. Companies need to support the investment and training of both male and female new leaders.

We need to examine the types of roles women are promoted to. Traditionally, women have received promotions into such historically female roles as heads of human resources or corporate social responsibility departments. Instead, promote women into roles of real decision-making, meaning they run budgets with profit generation or loss implications.

Now that we have climate, health, and social justice challenges, communities and investors want accountability. It is important that companies recognize the capacity women have been cultivating in these previously underappreciated roles. Companies reap the value of promoting women into seats with elevated importance and decision-making authority over the larger budgets now being allocated to these departments.

When assessing a company for how well it promotes women, make sure women are set up to be successful. In other words, women should not be selectively promoted into the most challenging contexts. Instead, they should enter into any context where their talents will be optimally utilized and where they will be positioned to be successful. If you want these promoted women to be successful and if you want to optimize their contributions to the company, it is essential to give them the benefits and pay packages that male colleagues receive. Sadly, the inverse is often the case. In a 2005 report, psychologists Michelle Ryan and Alex Haslam coined the term *glass cliff* when their study revealed that while more women were moved into positions of leadership, they were more likely than men to find themselves in risky operating contexts where they had to clean up messes usually left behind by male predecessors. There is an implied acknowledgment that times of crisis require female leadership traits, including collaborative leadership, ability to listen, taking the long view, and less appetite for unnecessary risk.[471] Male-dominated C-suites have a tendency to give women the messiest and most difficult promotions, perhaps to set them up to fail or because they are giving the plum promotions to people more like themselves. But there may be more sinister motivations as well. Consider the 2014 promotion of Mary Barra to CEO of General Motors, for example. Soon after her appointment, the company announced a massive car recall connected to an allegation that it had not corrected a problem linked to thirteen deaths. Observers asked about when the board knew about the problem and whether they had promoted a woman to be the "fall guy."[472]

In exploring how boards become more gender diverse, the Ryan and Haslam study reviewed the performance of FTSE 100 companies before and after the appointment of a male or female board member. The study revealed that during a period of overall stock market decline, those companies that appointed women to their boards were more likely to have experienced consistently bad performance in the preceding five months than those that appointed men.[473] As an investor, avoid companies that demonstrate this pattern.

DESIGN FOR WOMEN

Women make up half the population and, in many cases, make the purchasing decisions for their families and others in their lives. You will be rewarded if you invest in companies that design products that meet the needs of women— whether it's cars, cities, food, or health care. Because women are the majority users of most consumer products, they are closest to the problems, thus making them invaluable to any design team. Women need to be engaged at the design table and at every step of the innovation process. This includes women contributing input during the research phase to identify problems or opportunities, women engineers participating in the actual design, and female focus groups testing the marketing of new products. It also means female patients on advisory boards when scientists are designing new clinical trials. And not all women are the same—so you need more than one (ideally three or more) to provide input and innovation. Even if companies are designing a new product or technology specifically for men, chances are there is a blind spot in the design that women's input will help overcome.

It sometimes takes effort to bring women to the design table. Reaching out to a community, providing training, and building trust are all required elements of effectively bringing diverse input to product design. In addition to women on design teams, all innovators should constantly be considering how other diverse populations (by gender, race, disabilities, and so on) will access a product and how a failure to consider diverse populations could have negative consequences and create risk to the product and to the population (think crash test dummies and heart disease). Failure to fully consider how women and others will utilize a product creates risk to your investments—whatever service or product you are investing in.

VOTE FOR MORE WOMEN

We have cited several examples of the positive health and wealth results that have accrued to citizens who elect women to leadership positions, from village councils to heads of state. Considering the recent acceleration of dislocations and disruptions, we need to cast more votes for women at all levels of public governance—including school boards and local, regional, and country-level leadership. As investors, we should participate in investor statements and shareholder resolutions that demand more women in executive suites, capital-allocation roles, and boards of directors. We need more women because we are in a historical moment that demands female governance traits such as collaborative leadership, risk awareness, and the ability to see the long view.

Women are more likely to vote other women into corporate or government leadership, but men are beginning to understand that voting for women means voting for diverse viewpoints, for less risk-taking leadership, and for better health and wealth outcomes for citizens. Just as more men need to vote for more women officeholders, more women need to step up and run for governance positions. The most common word we hear when trying to get women to run for office is *ask*. Men proactively run for office, while women wait to be asked to do so.[474] Citizens, particularly male citizens, must work to cultivate environments that welcome women into the governance sphere and remove the confidence barrier to entry.

Fortunately, there is progress to report. In the public space, we have the greatest number of women country leaders and parliamentarians than at any other time.[475] Even though the percentage of women parliamentarians worldwide is still a dismally low 24.9%, this is significantly higher than the 11.7% of seats women held in 1997.[476] In the private sector, the global average of women on boards is getting better—sitting at 16.9% of global board seats according to 2018 data—mostly as a result of regulated mandates, as in the United Kingdom and the state of California, and now as a Securities and Exchange Commission–approved requirement for Nasdaq-listed companies.[477]

Mandates are good in instances when change is not going to happen, or at least not fast enough, but citizen action is even better. Male citizens can donate to female campaigns, volunteer time to canvass and talk to other male citizens, and show up at the polls and vote for women. Male investors can vote their shareholder proxies in ways that encourage female leadership at the corporate level. Women in governance positions will deliver better long-term results and thereby more wealth for individuals, sustained profitability for businesses, and greater sustainable growth for economies.

LISTEN TO WOMEN

This means inviting women to participate and having more than one woman in the conversation. If you listen to women and see the world through their eyes, better ways of investing will become apparent. Listening in the workplace is important at all levels—including listening to our female bosses, peers, and junior team members. According to David Smith and Brad Johnson in their book *Good Guys*, specific actions can promote women's voices in the workplace.[478] For example, including women in all work-connected gatherings and listening generously with the intention to understand. Ask clarifying questions when women are speaking, but don't interrupt with "mansplaining" (defined as "an explanation of something by a man, typically to a woman, in a manner that is regarded as condescending or patronizing"[479]). It's also important to literally make space for women in the room, and this requires increased awareness of when men are taking up more space, either physically or verbally.

Listening to women is important outside of the workplace as well. If you are a member of a local city council, neighborhood watch committee, or other such group, pay attention to who is in the room. Who is actively participating in the discussions and whose ideas are being listened to?

As we have shown, strong evidence indicates that when individuals with underrepresented identities are working in a group, it can take a minimum threshold of three of that type of person before they feel comfortable speaking and have their point of view taken into consideration.[480] If there is only one woman on a corporate board, in a legislative body, or on a senior leadership team, she is likely to serve as a token member, making the male members feel better about themselves for having a woman at the table but having little impact on outcomes. She will not be able to give optimum value.

TELL YOUR FRIENDS!

Men are essential to creating the cultural change that will be necessary to optimize talent across the capital markets. This is not a women's issue—it is everyone's issue. Those who have power must acknowledge the value of opening doors for others, be curious about the experience of others, and actively promote others' leadership in the workplace and beyond. Work to influence other men rather than succumb to peer pressure to conform to existing cultural norms.

There are two ways to tell your friends and influence a change in culture. The first is to share the information that we've presented in this book with your friends and family. Let them know that when women are closer to financial decision-making, they will effect a greater return on investment. Don't let this stay a well-kept secret. The other way to tell your friends is through your actions. Whether it's openly citing the work of a female colleague, speaking out against those who sexually harass or diminish female coworkers, or fundraising for female politicians on both local and national ballots, your actions will go a long way to change ingrained patterns of behaviors in our society.

Other important actions include directing your investment advisors to invest in more funds managed by women or screening your investment portfolio for companies that have more than three women on their boards. If we all do our part to influence our networks and communities, more women will be in positions of decision-making, especially financial decision-making, and we will all win with better health and wealth. We will all have more pie!

EPILOGUE

THROUGHOUT OUR WRITING DURING THE SUMMER months of 2021, we were impressed by the stories we've heard of intentional activity resulting in positive changes for women and girls and the communities, businesses, and countries they are actively strengthening. Stories of women's exemplary leadership during a global pandemic, accelerating climate disasters, and unrest caused by significant inequality are becoming everyday reading. A friend recently termed this momentum "an accelerated catch-up phase." As we wrap up our writing, it is fitting and important that we share and applaud the stories of these many positive shoots of progress.

For a long time, the focus has been on girls' limited access to education. With concerted efforts to balance the scales, we are witnessing improvements in the numbers of girls acquiring education, even in the most challenging contexts, from India to the United States.

In India, a determined male teacher found that many of his students, mostly female, were required to stay home to do chores and farm work. He developed technology to help them keep up with their schoolwork. He campaigned and successfully convinced the government of Maharashtra to adopt QR-coded textbooks, where the codes link to supplementary teaching materials, including teacher-generated videos to help students understand class content. This teacher who would not give up on his female students just won a $1 million prize as the world's most exceptional educator. Technological solutions such as QR-coded books will enable greater reach for female students in the most remote locations.[481]

In the United States, female students are graduating from college at higher rates across all levels, from associate degrees to doctorates. Starting in the 1970s, women have been gradually making gains. In 1970, 43% of college students and 9.6% of doctorate-level degree students were women; by the end of the 2020–2021 academic year, 59.5% of college students and 54% of doctorate-level degree students were women.[482] This is female talent that values collaboration, risk mitigation, and the long view and are more available for recruitment, retention, and sponsorship to the top rungs of business and governments. Just as important are efforts to make sure that there is infrastructure designed to prevent extreme swings of not having enough men around decision-making tables. It is the availability and inclusion of the diverse talent of men *and* women at all tables that are keys to driving more robust collaborative outcomes.

Similarly in financial services we are witnessing the intentional creation of space in important rooms and at exclusive tables. An August 2021 CNBC report highlighted how women and minorities were beginning to receive invitations to participate as underwriters in IPOs—a market dominated by white male networks. Diversity in the underwriting community democratizes financial markets as well as infuses differentiated sensibilities into the process. Everyone benefits within the companies that are going public, from their boards to their leadership and internal employee benefits structures.[483]

Astonishingly, some of the most repeated headlines emerging from the August 2021 return of Taliban leadership in Afghanistan are the ones lamenting the possible setback to the progress women and girls had made as students, entrepreneurs, and political actors. The situation is tragic, yet the focus on the strides women had made is heartening and a cause for celebrating them, hopefully signaling a recognition that their participation is vital to economic growth.

Overall, the shift in coverage to women as actors and solution-drivers and away from framing them as only victims and beneficiaries of action by others is momentous. This change in both the perception of and the actual role of women in all spheres will drive greater inclusion in the rooms that matter, especially in capital markets, and thereby facilitate individual health and wealth, global economic growth, and, yes, unlock higher returns and lower risk!

ACKNOWLEDGMENTS

I T TAKES SEVERAL VILLAGES TO WRITE A BOOK. FIRST, we want to thank some of the senior stateswomen of gender-focused investing—Jackie VanderBrug, Suzanne Biegel, and Joy Anderson—whose collaboration, wisdom, and passion inspire us every day. We also thank all those who helped us brainstorm our book's ideas, especially Carol Mitchell, Ed McKinley, Hugo Van Hung, Russ Siegelman, Nadine Burke-Harris, Brent Kessel, Tuti Scott, Andy Maack, Adam Ward, Michael Greenstein, James Manyika, David Press, Philippe Sachs, and the Oculus Forum. A huge thanks to those who helped with the research and editing, including Katherine Xiong, Sophie Clark, Isy Osubor, Charlotte Vargos, Jennifer Booker, Shelley Alpern, Maarten van Lieshout, Eleanor Levin, Jon McGoran, Anne Dubuisson, Stephen Power, and Ann Logue.

Patience is forever in debt to the amazing talent at and around Women of the World Endowment, who nurture the thesis and work of centralizing women as solution drivers to today's environmental, social, and governance challenges— Lili Forouraghi, Takuro Kimura, Lesley Ndhlovu, Junko Yoda, Philippe Sachs, Kwame Lewis, Atul Mehta, Melanie Warfield, Mindy Possof, Jeff Nasser, Maria Skuratovskaya, Angela Lumanau, Marty Nealon, Pamela Coleman, Julie Katzman, Katie Hoff, Pooja Eppanappally, Michael Notaro, Megan Torres, Amanda Progress, and Danielle Burt— whose invaluable support fueled the ideas and content in this book. Patience's gratitude is boundless for the love and space that her sons Tayo and Tendai, and her best friend and husband, Mark Ball, gave so this book could be written.

Ruth is deeply grateful to her extraordinary team at the Tara Health Foundation who gave her the space and support to write, including Elise Belusa, Tenesha Duncan, Ellen George, Rivka Gordon, Emiko Higashi, Iris Kuo, Tim Loui, and Jen Stark. Thanks and appreciation also go to Mary Foust and Alena Meeker at Merrill, who jumped into the gender-focused investing space with transformative curiosity, enthusiasm, and expertise. Every day they demonstrate that you can make tons of money without compromising values. Ruth especially thanks her husband, Glenn Barnes, for his coaching, wisdom, and loving support, and to her darling daughter, Madeline, who didn't laugh or say it was crazy that her mother was going to write a book.

NOTES

Introduction

1   Milton Friedman and Rose Friedman, *Free to Choose: A Personal Statement* (New York: Harcourt, 1990), 13.

2   Jena McGregor, "More Women at the Top, Higher Returns," *Washington Post*, September 24, 2014, https://www.washingtonpost.com/news/on-leadership/wp/2014/09/24/more-women-at-the-top-higher-returns/; Brande Stellings, "Female Board Members Are Good for Business," *The New York Times*, April 1, 2015, https://www.nytimes.com/roomfordebate/2015/04/01/the-effect-of-women-on-corporate-boards/female-board-members-are-good-for-business.

3   Emma Hinchliffe, "The Female CEOs on This Year's Fortune 500 Just Broke Three All-Time Records," *Fortune*, June 2, 2021, https://fortune.com/2021/06/02/female-ceos-fortune-500-2021-women-ceo-list-roz-brewer-walgreens-karen-lynch-cvs-thasunda-brown-duckett-tiaa/.

4   "Women Make Up Just 14 Per Cent of Partners at UK Private

Equity Firms and Hedge Funds," Private Equity Wire, August 31, 2018, https://www.privateequitywire.co.uk/email/267911; Karen Firestone, "When Will We See More Gender Equality in Investing?," *Harvard Business Review*, March 25, 2019, https://hbr.org/2019/03/when-will-we-see-more-gender-equality-in-investing; "Venture Capital and Entrepreneurship," Harvard Kennedy School Women and Public Policy Program, accessed December 18, 2021, https://wappp.hks.harvard.edu/venture-capital-and-entrepreneurship.

5   Lauren Hirsch, "The Business Case for Boardroom Diversity," *The New York Times*, January 23, 2021, https://www.nytimes.com/2021/01/23/business/dealbook/diversity-board-directors.html.

6   Derek Thompson, "Why Women Prefer Working Together (and Why Men Prefer Working Alone)," *The Atlantic*, August 21, 2013, https://www.theatlantic.com/business/archive/2013/08/why-women-prefer-working-together-and-why-men-prefer-working-alone/278888/.

7   Christine Lagarde, "Ten Years After Lehman—Lessons Learned and Challenges Ahead," *IMF Blog* (blog), September 5, 2018, https://blogs.imf.org/2018/09/05/ten-years-after-lehman-lessons-learned-and-challenges-ahead/.

8   Durreen Shahnaz, "Is White Liberalism Taking Over Impact Investing?," *Impact Investment Exchange* (blog), December 3, 2019, https://iixglobal.com/is-white-liberalism-taking-over-impact-investing/.

9   Steven Pinker, *Enlightenment Now: The Case for Reason, Science, Humanism, and Progress* (New York: Viking, 2018), 28.

Chapter 1

10 Lisa Abeyta, "Women Now Make Up Almost 5 Percent of Investors in the U.S.," *Inc.*, October 23, 2020, https://www.inc.com/lisa-abeyta/women-now-make-up-almost-five-percent-of-investors-in-us.html.

11 "Improving Patient and Worker Safety: Opportunities for Synergy, Collaboration, and Innovation" (Oakbrook Terrace,

IL: The Joint Commission, November 2012), 51.

12 Robert Carden, "Behavioral Economics Show That Women Tend to Make Better Investments than Men," *The Washington Post*, October 11, 2013, https://www.washingtonpost.com/business/behavioral-economics-show-that-women-tend-to-make-better-investments-than-men/2013/10/10/5347f40e-2d50-11e3-97a3-ff2758228523_story.html.

13 Carden, "Behavioral Economics Show"; "Women Are Leading the Charge for Environmental, Social and Governance (ESG) Investing in the U.S. amid Growing Demand for Responsible Investing Solutions," RBC Wealth Management, April 6, 2021, https://www.rbcwealthmanagement.com/en-us/newsroom/2021-04-06/women-are-leading-the-charge-for-environmental-social-and-governance-esg-investing-in-the-us-amid-growing-demand-for-responsible-investing-solutions.

14 Bryan Caplan and Zach Weinersmith, *Open Borders: The Science and Ethics of Immigration* (New York: First Second, 2019).

15 Heather Long, "2020 Is the Summer of Booming Home Sales—and Evictions," *The Washington Post*, July 27, 2020, https://www.washingtonpost.com/business/2020/07/27/housing-inequality-coronavirus/.

16 Wayne Duggan, "Collaboration and Capitalism: Barron's Wealth Gap Event Speakers Address American Financial Inequities," Benzinga, June 23, 2021, https://dev.sparknewswire.com/newsfeed/collaboration-and-capitalism-barrons-wealth-gap-event-speakers-address-american-financial-inequities; Calvin G. Butler, "Moving from Talk to Action," Panel Discussion, The Wealth Gap, 2021, https://www.barrons.com/video/moving-from-talk-to-action-the-wealth-gap/5646F73E-C99C-4328-8256-F5DB10703FBC.html.

17 Butler, "Moving from Talk to Action."

18 "The World's Largest Retirement Funds in 2021," *Pensions & Investments*, September 6, 2021, https://www.pionline.com/interactive/worlds-largest-retirement-funds-2021; Margaryta Kirakosian, "World's Largest Asset Owner Invests €2.4bn in

Gender Diversity Index," CityWire Selector, December 21, 2020, https://citywireselector.com/news/worlds-largest-asset-owner-invests-2-4bn-in-gender-diversity-index/a1441852; Rebecca Henderson et al., "Should a Pension Fund Try to Change the World? Inside GPIF's Embrace of ESG," Harvard Business School, February 1, 2020.

19 Rebecca Henderson and George Serafeim, "Should a Pension Fund Try to Change the World?," Cold Call: Inside A Case Study, *Harvard Business Review*, accessed December 29, 2021, https://hbr.org/podcast/2019/08/should-a-pension-fund-try-to-change-the-world.

20 Jonathan Woetzel et al., "How Advancing Women's Equality Can Add $12 Trillion to Global Growth," McKinsey Global Institute, September 1, 2015, https://www.mckinsey.com/featured-insights/employment-and-growth/how-advancing-womens-equality-can-add-12-trillion-to-global-growth.

21 Woetzel et al., "How Advancing Women's Equality."

22 Beth Ann Bovino and Jason Gold, "The Key to Unlocking U.S. GDP Growth? Women," S&P Global, October 1, 2018, https://www.spglobal.com/en/research-insights/featured/the-key-to-unlocking-u-s-gdp-growth-women.

23 Bovino and Gold, "Key to Unlocking?"

24 Shelby R. Buckman et al., "The Economic Gains from Equity," Working Paper, Federal Reserve Bank of San Francisco, April 2021, 17, https://www.frbsf.org/economic-research/publications/working-papers/2021/11/.

25 Buckman et al., "Economic Gains from Equity."

26 Christine Lagarde and Jonathan D. Ostry, "Economic Gains from Gender Inclusion: Even Greater than You Thought," *International Monetary Fund Blog* (blog), November 28, 2018, https://blogs.imf.org/2018/11/28/economic-gains-from-gender-inclusion-even-greater-than-you-thought/.

27 Lagarde and Ostry, "Economic Gains."

28 Lagarde and Ostry, "Economic Gains."

29 Lagarde and Ostry, "Economic Gains."

30 Haim Israel et al., "Everybody Counts! Diversity & Inclusion

Primer," Bank of America, March 4, 2021, https://business.
bofa.com/content/dam/boamlimages/documents/articles/
ID21_0317/everybody_counts_DI_report.pdf.

31 *Credit Suisse Gender 3000 Report 2019* (Credit Suisse,
October 10, 2019), 20–21, https://www.credit-suisse.com/
about-us-news/en/articles/news-and-expertise/cs-gender-3000-
report-2019-201910.html.

32 Jeff Green, "Women's Gains Push Majority of S&P 500
Boards into the 30% Club," *Bloomberg*, August 16, 2021,
https://www.bloomberg.com/news/articles/2021-08-16/
women-s-gains-push-majority-of-s-p-500-boards-into-the-
30-club.

33 *Credit Suisse Gender 3000 Report 2019*, 20–21.

34 *Credit Suisse Gender 3000 Report 2019*, 21.

35 Israel et al., "Everybody Counts! Diversity & Inclusion Primer."

36 Cedric Herring, "Does Diversity Pay? Race, Gender, and
the Business Case for Diversity," *American Sociological
Review*, April 1, 2009, https://journals.sagepub.com/doi/
abs/10.1177/000312240907400203.

37 Rocio Lorenzo and Martin Reeves, "How and Where Diversity
Drives Financial Performance," *Harvard Business Review*,
January 30, 2018, https://hbr.org/2018/01/how-and-where-
diversity-drives-financial-performance.

38 Rocío Lorenzo et al., "How Diverse Leadership Teams Boost
Innovation," Boston Consulting Group, January 2018, https://
www.bcg.com/publications/2018/how-diverse-leadership-
teams-boost-innovation.

39 Paul Gompers and Silpa Kovvali, "The Other Diversity
Dividend," *Harvard Business Review*, August 2018, https://hbr.
org/2018/07/the-other-diversity-dividend.

40 Gompers and Kovvali, "Other Diversity Dividend."

41 Gompers and Kovvali, "Other Diversity Dividend."

42 Gompers and Kovvali, "Other Diversity Dividend."

43 "Facts and Figures: Women's Leadership and Political
Participation," UN Women, accessed December 18,
2021, https://www.unwomen.org/en/what-we-do/

leadership-and-political-participation/facts-and-figures; Raghabendra Chattopadhyay and Esther Duflo, "Women as Policy Makers: Evidence from a Randomized Policy Experiment in India," *Econometrica* 72, no. 5 (September 2004): 1409–43.

44 Kathleen A. Bratton and Leonard P. Ray, "Descriptive Representation, Policy Outcomes, and Municipal Day-Care Coverage in Norway," *American Journal of Political Science* 46, no. 2 (2002): 428–37.

45 Keith Barry, "The Crash Test Bias: How Male-Focused Testing Puts Female Drivers at Risk," *Consumer Reports*, October 23, 2019, https://www.consumerreports.org/car-safety/crash-test-bias-how-male-focused-testing-puts-female-drivers-at-risk/.

46 "Fatality Facts 2019: Males and Females," IIHS-HLDI, accessed December 18, 2021, https://www.iihs.org/topics/fatality-statistics/detail/males-and-females.

47 Katherine Shaver, "Female Dummy Makes Her Mark on Male-Dominated Crash Tests," *The Washington Post*, March 25, 2012, https://www.washingtonpost.com/local/trafficandcommuting/female-dummy-makes-her-mark-on-male-dominated-crash-tests/2012/03/07/gIQANBLjaS_story.html; Caroline Criado-Perez, "The Deadly Truth About a World Built for Men—from Stab Vests to Car Crashes," *The Guardian*, February 23, 2019, https://www.theguardian.com/lifeandstyle/2019/feb/23/truth-world-built-for-men-car-crashes.

48 Charles J. Kahane, "Injury Vulnerability and Effectiveness of Occupant Protection Technologies for Older Occupants and Women," National Highway Traffic Safety Administration, May 2013, https://crashstats.nhtsa.dot.gov/api/public/viewpublication/811766.

49 Shaver, "Female Dummy Makes Her Mark."

50 Criado-Perez, "Deadly Truth."

51 Criado-Perez, "Deadly Truth."

52 "49 CFR § 571.208 - Standard No. 208; Occupant Crash Protection." (1984).

53 "Counts of Frontal Air Bag Related Fatalities and Seriously Injured Persons," National Highway Traffic Safety Administration, January 2009, "Counts of Frontal Air Bag Related Fatalities and Seriously Injured Persons" (National Highway Traffic Safety Administration, July 1, 2007).

54 "Counts of Frontal Air Bag Related Fatalities."

55 "Counts of Frontal Air Bag Related Fatalities."

56 Unni Eikeseth, "Gender Equality for Crash Test Dummies, Too," ScienceNordic, January 24, 2013, https://sciencenordic. com/cars-and-traffic-crash-test-dummies-forskningno/gender-equality-for-crash-test-dummies-too/1381623.

57 Eikeseth, "Gender Equality."

58 Barry, "Crash Test Bias."

59 Laura Castañón, "Most Biomedical Research Is Done on Male Animals. That's a Public Health Problem," *News @ Northeastern*, May 30, 2019, https://news.northeastern. edu/2019/05/30/most-biomedical-research-is-done-male-animals-thats-a-public-health-problem/.

60 Anne Hamilton Dougherty, "Gender Balance in Cardiovascular Research," *Texas Heart Institute Journal* 38, no. 2 (2011): 148–50.

61 "The Coronary Drug Project," *Circulation* 47, no. 3s1 (March 1, 1973): I–1; "Final Report on the Aspirin Component of the Ongoing Physicians' Health Study," *New England Journal of Medicine*, July 20, 1989, 129–35.

62 Faustino R. Pérez-López et al., "Gender Differences in Cardiovascular Disease: Hormonal and Biochemical Influences," *Reproductive Sciences* (Thousand Oaks, Calif.) 17, no. 6 (June 2010): 511–31.

63 "Appropriations (Section 1)," National Institutes of Health (NIH), March 25, 2015, https://www.nih.gov/about-nih/what-we-do/nih-almanac/appropriations-section-1; "Bernadine Healy," Changing the Face of Medicine, updated June 3, 2015, https://cfmedicine.nlm.nih.gov/physicians/biography_145.html.

64 Aruna D. Pradhan et al., "Inflammatory Biomarkers,

Hormone Replacement Therapy, and Incident Coronary Heart Disease: Prospective Analysis from the Women's Health Initiative Observational Study," *Journal of the American Medical Association* 288, no. 8 (August 28, 2002): 980–87.

65 Clare J. Taylor et al., "National Trends in Heart Failure Mortality in Men and Women, United Kingdom, 2000–2017," *European Journal of Heart Failure* 23, no. 1 (September 6, 2020): 3–12.

66 Sonya Burgess, Elizabeth Shaw, and Sarah Zaman, "Women in Cardiology," *Circulation* 139, no. 8 (February 19, 2019): 1001–2; Laxmi S. Mehta et al., "Current Demographic Status of Cardiologists in the United States," *JAMA Cardiology* 4, no. 10 (October 1, 2019): 1029–33.

67 Jacques E. Rossouw et al., "Risks and Benefits of Estrogen plus Progestin in Healthy Postmenopausal Women: Principal Results from the Women's Health Initiative Randomized Controlled Trial," *JAMA* 288, no. 3 (July 17, 2002): 321–33; "Researchers—Principal Investigators," Women's Health Initiative.

68 Lean Six Sigma, "Lean Six Sigma for Manufacturing," Lean Six Sigma Institute, accessed December 19, 2021; Toyota Motor Corporation, "Toyota Production System," Toyota Motor Corporation Official Global Website, accessed December 19, 2021, https://global.toyota/en/company/vision-and-philosophy/production-system/.

69 Peter Lazes and Marie Rudden, *From the Ground Up: How Frontline Staff Can Save America's Healthcare* (Oakland, CA: Berrett-Koehler Publishers, 2020), 8.

70 "Engage Patients to Help Shape Your Clinical Research," National Institute for Health Research, accessed December 19, 2021, https://www.nihr.ac.uk/explore-nihr/industry/pecd.htm.

71 Susan Birk, "Women in Leadership: Hardwiring the Culture," *Healthcare Executive*, December 2019; Lydia Ramsey Pflanzer, "There's Something Missing from One of the Largest Healthcare Investor Meetings of the Year," *Business Insider*, January 10, 2017; Bill Pieroni, "Increasing Gender Diversity

in Insurance Leadership," Spencer Stuart, March 2019, https://www.spencerstuart.com/research-and-insight/increasing-gender-diversity-in-insurance-leadership.

72 Pflanzer, "There's Something Missing."

73 Vicki Phillips, "What Would a City Look like if It Were Designed Entirely by and for Women? These Places Offer a Glimpse," *Forbes*, March 22, 2021, https://www.forbes.com/sites/vickiphillips/2021/03/22/what-would-a-city-look-like-if-it-were-designed-entirely-by-and-for-women-these-places-offer-a-glimpse/?sh=19aaae67367e.

74 Jennifer Gardner and Larissa Begault, "How Better Urban Planning Can Improve Gender Equality," *Behavioral Scientist*, April 9, 2019, https://behavioralscientist.org/how-better-urban-planning-can-improve-gender-equality/.

75 "Maputo Youth Aim to Make the City Safer with Photography," *Africa Times*, March 8, 2019, https://africatimes.com/2019/03/08/maputo-youth-aim-to-make-the-city-safer-with-photography/.

76 Kalpana Viswanath, "SafetiPin: A Tool to Build Safer Cities for Women," *The Asia Foundation*, May 11, 2016, https://asiafoundation.org/2016/05/11/safetipin-tool-build-safer-cities-women/.

77 Safetipin, accessed December 19, 2021, https://safetipin.com.

78 Safetipin.

79 Balgis Osman-Elasha, "Women . . . in the Shadow of Climate Change," United Nations, accessed December 19, 2021, https://www.un.org/en/chronicle/article/womenin-shadow-climate-change.

80 Trish Glazebrook, "Women and Climate Change: A Case-Study from Northeast Ghana," *Hypatia* 26, no. 4 (2011): 763.

81 Glazebrook, "Women and Climate Change," 770–71.

82 Glazebrook, "Women and Climate Change," 765–68.

83 Glazebrook, "Women and Climate Change," 767.

84 Corinne Post, Boris Lokshin, and Christophe Boone, "Research: Adding Women to the C-Suite Changes How

Companies Think," *Harvard Business Review*, April 6, 2021, https://hbr.org/2021/04/research-adding-women-to-the-c-suite-changes-how-companies-think.

85 Judy B. Rosener, "Ways Women Lead," *Harvard Business Review*, November 1, 1990, https://hbr.org/1990/11/ways-women-lead.

86 Joan Michelson, "Why Choosing Women as Leaders Reduces Risk," *Forbes*, June 24, 2021.

87 Post, Lokshin, and Boone, "Adding Women to the C-Suite."

88 Post, Lokshin, and Boone, "Adding Women to the C-Suite."

89 Carol Vallone Mitchell, *Collaboration Code: How Men Lead Culture Change and Nurture Tomorrow's Leaders* (Franklin, TN: Post Hill Press, 2021).

90 Jane Dudman, "Female Leaders Make a Real Difference. Covid May Be the Proof," *The Guardian*, December 16, 2020, https://www.theguardian.com/society/2020/dec/16/female-leaders-make-a-real-difference-covid-may-be-the-proof.

91 https://www.forbes.com/sites/shaheenajanjuhajivrajeurope/2020/05/20/ohisalo-covid-19-finland/?sh=436ebfc42561 HYPERLINK "https://www.forbes.com/sites/shaheenajanju-hajivrajeurope/" Shaheena Janjuha-Jivraj May 20, 2020

92 Amanda Taub, "Why Are Women-Led Nations Doing Better with Covid-19?," *The New York Times*, May 15, 2020, https://www.nytimes.com/2020/05/15/world/coronavirus-women-leaders.html.

93 Nara Raman, Yosuke Kido, and Ioana Hussaida, "The Land of the Long White Cloud: Turning New Zealand's Recovery into Sustained Growth," International Monetary Fund News, May 27, 2021, https://www.imf.org/en/News/Articles/2021/05/25/na052521-the-land-of-the-long-white-cloud-turning-new-zea-lands-recovery-into-sustained-growth.

94 Sarah Harman and Carlo Angerer, "How Iceland Became a Covid-19 Success Story," NBC News, March 15, 2021, https://www.yahoo.com/now/test-trace-trust-iceland-became-083109585.html.

95 Raman, Kido, and Hussaida, "Land of the Long White Cloud."

96 https://www.dw.com/en/coronavirus-finland-sweden-role-model/a-55664117.

97 https://www.oecd.org/sdd/its/Finland-COVID-Report-May-2021.pdf FINLAND: ROAD TO RECOVERY AFTER COVID-19.

98 "Iceland: Increase Competition and Economic Diversification to Support the Recovery from COVID-19, Says OECD," *OECD*, July 7, 2021, https://www.oecd.org/newsroom/iceland-increase-competition-and-economic-diversifica-tion-to-support-the-recovery-from-covid-19-says-oecd.htm.

99 Carlos Caceres, Mai Chi Dao, and Aiko Mineshima, "Beyond the Pandemic: Five Charts on Germany's Economic Recovery Plan," International Monetary Fund News, accessed December 19, 2021, https://www.imf.org/en/News/Articles/2021/07/13/na071521-beyond-the-pandemic-five-charts-on-germanys-economic-recovery-plan.

100 "Cumulative Confirmed COVID-19 Deaths," Our World in Data, accessed December 20, 2021, https://ourworld-indata.org/grapher/cumulative-covid-deaths-region; "WHO Coronavirus (COVID-19) Dashboard," World Health Organization, accessed December 20, 2021, https://covid19.who.int; "COVID Live—Coronavirus Statistics," Worldometer, accessed December 20, 2021, https://www.worldometers.info/coronavirus/.

101 Inter-Parliamentary Union, ed., *Equality in Politics: A Survey of Women and Men in Parliaments*, Reports and Documents, no. 54 (Geneva: Inter-Parliamentary Union, 2008), 62.

102 Inter-Parliamentary Union, *Equality in Politics*, 70.

103 Julia Kollewe, "Covid Vaccine Technology Pioneer: 'I Never Doubted It Would Work,'" *The Guardian*, November 21, 2020, https://www.theguardian.com/science/2020/nov/21/covid-vaccine-technology-pioneer-i-never-doubted-it-would-work.

104 Gina Kolata, "Kati Kariko Helped Shield the World from the Coronavirus," *The New York Times*, April 8, 2021, https://www.nytimes.com/2021/04/08/health/coronavirus-mrna-kariko.html.

105 "Prof Sarah Gilbert: The Woman Who Designed the Oxford Vaccine," BBC News, November 23, 2020, https://www.bbc.com/news/uk-55043551.

106 Norah O'Donnell, "Meet the Women at Forefront of COVID-19 Vaccine Development," CBS News, April 1, 2021, https://www.cbsnews.com/news/covid-vaccine-nita-patel-kizzmekia-corbett/.

107 Trinidad Beleche et al., "COVID-19 Vaccine Hesitancy: Demographic Factors, Geographic Patterns, and Changes over Time," Office of the Assistant Secretary for Planning and Evaluation, U.S. Department of Health and Human Services, May 2021, https://aspe.hhs.gov/sites/default/files/private/pdf/265341/aspe-ib-vaccine-hesitancy.pdf.

108 Kizzmekia Corbett (@KizzyPHD), 2021, "1/n: I'm getting my @moderna_tx booster tomorrow. Following the @US_FDA & @CDCgov's newest guidance that US citizens like myself (18+, not high risk, 10 months after 2nd dose) *may* acquire a booster, I used the following personal guide to make the choice," Twitter, November 20, 2021, 10:10 p.m.; Kizzmekia Corbett (@KizzyPHD), 2021, "*remixxxx* Can you tell me how to get . . . how to get . . . (vaccinated on) @sesame-street? Grab the whole family tomorrow (11/6) at 8:30am to get many of your questions answered about the newly authorized COVID-19 vaccine for 5-11 year olds! @CNN," Twitter, November 5, 2021, 4:49 p.m.; Kizzmekia Corbett (@KizzyPHD), 2020, "Our (co-inventors @McLellan_Lab) COVID-19 vaccine (spike delivered by @moderna_tx's mRNA) was just injected into the 1st human in phase 1 trial, only 66 days after viral sequence release . . . a testament to rapid vaccine development for emerging diseases," Twitter, March 16, 2020, 1:10 p.m.

109 "Health Equity Considerations and Racial and Ethnic Minority Groups," Centers for Disease Control and Prevention, November 30, 2021, https://www.cdc.gov/coronavirus/2019-ncov/community/health-equity/race-ethnicity.html.

110 Heidi Ledford and Ewen Callaway, "Pioneers of Revolutionary

CRISPR Gene Editing Win Chemistry Nobel," *Nature*, October 7, 2020, https://www.nature.com/articles/d41586-020-02765-9.

111 Damian Garde and Jonathan Saltzman, "The Story of MRNA: How a Once-Dismissed Idea Became a Leading Technology in the Covid Vaccine Race," *Stat+*, November 10, 2020, https://www.statnews.com/2020/11/10/the-story-of-mrna-how-a-once-dismissed-idea-became-a-leading-technology-in-the-covid-vaccine-race/.

112 Elsa Estevez, "Portugal: Leapfrogging Digital Transformation," CAF Development Bank of Latin America, July 14, 2021, https://www.caf.com/en/knowledge/views/2021/07/portugal-leapfrogging-digital-transformation/.

113 Carlos Santiso, "What We Can Learn from the Women of E-Portugal," Apolitical, January 25, 2021, https://apolitical.co/solution-articles/en/learn-women-e-portugal.

114 "Uber Invests over €90 Million in Lisbon," *The Portugal News*, September 17, 2021, https://www.theportugalnews.com/news/2021-09-17/uber-invests-over-90-million-in-lisbon/62465.

115 "SIMPLEX," Observatory of Public Sector Innovation, accessed December 20, 2021, https://www.oecd-opsi.org/innovations/simplex/.

116 "Justiça + Próxima 20|23: Plano de Modernização Da Justiça," Justiça + Próxima, accessed December 20, 2021, https://justicamaisproxima.justica.gov.pt/en/.

117 Minda Zetlin, "Malcolm Gladwell Says the Post-Pandemic World Will Be 'a Much Better Place,'" *Inc.*, May 8, 2021, https://www.inc.com/minda-zetlin/malcolm-gladwell-post-pandemic-covid-optimism-adobe-summit.html.

118 Zetlin, "Malcolm Gladwell Says."

119 Fridays for Future, accessed December 20, 2021, https://fridaysforfuture.org.

120 Zetlin, "Malcolm Gladwell Says."

121 Emily Guy Birken, "Why Women Are Better Investors," *Forbes Advisor*, March 30, 2021, https://www.forbes.com/advisor/

investing/woman-better-investors/.

122 Jie Chen et al., "Research: When Women Are on Boards, Male CEOs Are Less Overconfident," *Harvard Business Review*, September 12, 2019, https://hbr.org/2019/09/research-when-women-are-on-boards-male-ceos-are-less-overconfident.

123 Post, Lokshin, and Boone, "Adding Women to the C-Suite."

124 Nerilee Hing et al., *A Comparative Study of Men and Women Gamblers in Victoria* (Victorian Responsible Gambling Foundation, November 2014), https://responsiblegambling.vic.gov.au/documents/76/Research-report-comparative-study-of-men-and-women-gamblers.pdf.

125 Hing et al., *Comparative Study*.

126 Mike Johnson, "Do Women Make Better Gamblers than Men?," *Gambling News*, October 27, 2020, https://www.gamblingnews.com/blog/do-women-make-better-gamblers-than-men/.

127 Chen et al., "Research: When Women Are on Boards."

128 Fitriya Fauzi, Abdul Basyith, and Poh-Ling Ho, "Women on Boardroom: Does It Create Risk?," *Cogent Economics & Finance* 5, no. 1 (May 10, 2017).

129 Post, Lokshin, and Boone, "Adding Women to the C-Suite."

130 "The Story of Silent Spring," NRDC, August 13, 2015, https://www.nrdc.org/stories/story-silent-spring.

131 "The Story of Silent Spring."

132 Nicholas Gilmore, "The Deafening Criticism Against Silent Spring," *The Saturday Evening Post*, September 27, 2017, https://www.saturdayeveningpost.com/2017/09/deafening-criticism-silent-spring/; Edwin Diamond, "The Myth of the 'Pesticide Menace,'" *The Saturday Evening Post*, September 28, 1963, https://www.saturdayeveningpost.com/reprints/the-myth-of-the-pesticide-menace/.

133 "Story of Silent Spring."

134 "DDT—A Brief History and Status," United States Environmental Protection Agency, January 7, 2014.

135 "SASB Standards," SASB, accessed December 20, 2021, https://www.sasb.org/standards/.

136 Bobby Allyn, "'The Computer Got It Wrong': How Facial Recognition Led to False Arrest of Black Man," NPR, June 24, 2020, https://www.npr.org/2020/06/24/882683463/the-computer-got-it-wrong-how-facial-recognition-led-to-a-false-arrest-in-michig.

137 Alex Najibi, "Racial Discrimination in Face Recognition Technology," *Science in the News | Harvard University* (blog), October 24, 2020, https://sitn.hms.harvard.edu/flash/2020/racial-discrimination-in-face-recognition-technology/.

138 "Algorithmic Justice League—Unmasking AI Harms and Biases," Algorithmic Justice League, accessed December 20, 2021, https://www.ajl.org.

139 Karen Hao, "We Read the Paper That Forced Timnit Gebru out of Google. Here's What It Says," *MIT Technology Review*, December 4, 2020, https://www.technologyreview.com/2020/12/04/1013294/google-ai-ethics-research-paper-forced-out-timnit-gebru/.

140 Joseph R. Gregory, "Margaret Thatcher, 'Iron Lady' Who Set Britain on New Course, Dies at 87," *The New York Times*, April 8, 2013, https://www.nytimes.com/2013/04/09/world/europe/former-prime-minister-margaret-thatcher-of-britain-has-died.html.

141 "Margaret Thatcher: Leadership Skills of the Iron Lady," Informa Connect, November 25, 2013, https://www.informa.com.au/insight/margaret-thatcher-leadership-skills-of-the-iron-lady/.

142 https://www.intelligentchange.com/blogs/read/is-masculine-or-feminine-energy-your-strength

143 Daphna Joel et al., "Sex Beyond the Genitalia: The Human Brain Mosaic," *Proceedings of the National Academy of Sciences* 112, no. 50 (December 15, 2015): 15468–73.

Chapter 2

144 *Gender Equality in the U.S.* (Equileap, December 2020), 7, https://equileap.com/wp-content/uploads/2020/12/Equileap_US_Report_2020.pdf.

145 *Gender Equality in the U.S.*

146 Katie Abouzahr et al., "Why Women-Owned Startups Are a Better Bet," BCG Global, July 30, 2020, https://www.bcg.com/publications/2018/why-women-owned-startups-are-better-bet; Elijah Owens, "Female-Inclusive Investment Committees Are Outperforming Their Peers," Chief Investment Officer, July 2, 2019, https://www.ai-cio.com/news/female-inclusive-investment-committees-outper-forming-peers/; Lois Joy, Harvey M. Wagner, and Sriram Narayanan, "The Bottom Line: Corporate Performance and Women's Representation on Boards," Catalyst, October 15, 2007, https://www.catalyst.org/research/the-bottom-line-cor-porate-performance-and-womens-representation-on-boards/; "IFC Banking on Women Business Case Update," Financial Alliance for Women, 2020, https://financialallianceforwomen.org/download/ifc-banking-on-women-business-case-update/.

147 Syed Zamberi Ahmad and Afida Mastura Muhammad Arif, "Strengthening Access to Finance for Women-Owned SMEs in Developing Countries," International Finance Corporation, October 2011.

148 "The XX Factor: A Framework and Guidebook for Improving the Lives of Women and Girls," Center for High Impact Philanthropy, University of Pennsylvania, accessed December 20, 2021, https://www.impact.upenn.edu/toolkits/the-xx-factor/.

149 "Invest Your Values," As You Sow, accessed December 20, 2021, https://www.asyousow.org/invest-your-values.

150 *Perspectives from Women of Impact: Redefining Legacy* (UBS, 2019), 6.

151 Aye M. Soe, "The Financial Future Is Female," S&P Global, March 2019, https://www.spglobal.com/en/research-insights/featured/the-financial-future-is-female.

152 Anna Zakrzewski et al., *Managing the Next Decade of Women's Wealth* (BCG Global, April 2020), 3, https://image-src.bcg.com/Images/BCG-Managing-the-Next-Decade-of-Womens-Wealth-Apr-2020_tcm9-243208.pdf.

153 *Perspectives from Women of Impact: Redefining Legacy*, 6.

154 Owens, "Female-Inclusive Investment Committees."

155 Owens, "Female-Inclusive Investment Committees."

156 Owens, "Female-Inclusive Investment Committees."

157 "Women in Alternative Investments: Building Momentum in 2013 and Beyond," Rothstein Kass Institute, December 2012.

158 "Vanguard Examines 401(k) Behavior/Outcome Gender Paradox," Vanguard, November 3, 2015, https://pressroom. vanguard.com/content/news/Press_Release_Women_and_DC_ plans_CRR_paper_110315.html.

159 Meredith Jones, *Women of the Street: Why Female Money Managers Generate Higher Returns (and How You Can Too)* (New York: Springer, 2015), 9.

160 "The Changemaker Series: Improving Investment Financial and Impact Performance through Diversity," Women of the World Endowment, November 19, 2021, https://www. youtube.com/watch?v=r86AyLHGpVo.

161 Graph data is from Kristin Hull, PhD, Nia Impact Capital.

162 "2020 Global Board Diversity Tracker: Who's Really on Board?," Egon Zehnder, accessed December 20, 2021, https:// www.egonzehnder.com/global-board-diversity-tracker; Jasmin Joecks, Kerstin Pull, and Karin Vetter, "Gender Diversity in the Boardroom and Firm Performance: What Exactly Constitutes a 'Critical Mass?,'" *Journal of Business Ethics* 118, no. 1 (November 21, 2012): 61; V. W. Kramer et al., "Critical Mass on Corporate Boards: Why Three or More Women Enhance Governance," *Directors Monthly* 31 (January 1, 2007).

163 Renée B. Adams and Daniel Ferreira, "Women in the Boardroom and Their Impact on Governance and Performance," *Journal of Financial Economics* 94 (August 4, 2009): 292–93.

164 Joy, Wagner, and Narayanan, "Bottom Line"; "Gender Diversity and Corporate Performance," Credit Suisse, August 2012.

165 Vivian Hunt et al., "Delivering Through Diversity," McKinsey & Company, January 2018, https://www.mckinsey.com/

business-functions/people-and-organizational-performance/
our-insights/delivering-through-diversity.

166 Mark Misercola, "Higher Returns with Women in
Decision-Making Positions," Credit Suisse, March 10, 2016,
https://www.credit-suisse.com/about-us-news/en/articles/
news-and-expertise/higher-returns-with-women-in-decision-
making-positions-201610.html.

167 Anita Williams Woolley et al., "Evidence for a Collective
Intelligence Factor in the Performance of Human Groups,"
Science 330, no. 6004 (October 29, 2010): 686–88.

168 Sonali Basak and Jeff Green, "Female CFOs Brought in $1.8
Trillion More than Male Peers," *Bloomberg*, October 16, 2019,
https://www.bloomberg.com/news/articles/2019-10-16/
female-cfos-brought-in-1-8-trillion-more-than-male-peers.

169 Basak and Green, "Female CFOs Brought."

170 Daniel J. Sandberg, *When Women Lead, Firms Win*
(S&P Global, October 16, 2019), https://www.spglobal.
com/_division_assets/images/special-editorial/iif-2019/
whenwomenlead_.pdf.

171 Sandberg, *When Women Lead, Firms Win*.

172 Alexander Osipovich and Akane Otani, "Nasdaq Seeks
Board-Diversity Rule That Most Listed Firms Don't Meet,"
The Wall Street Journal, December 1, 2020, https://www.wsj.
com/articles/nasdaq-proposes-board-diversity-rule-for-listed-
companies-11606829244.

173 Cydney Posner, "SEC Approves Nasdaq 'Comply-or-Explain'
Proposal for Board Diversity," Harvard Law School Forum
on Corporate Governance, August 26, 2021, https://corpgov.
law.harvard.edu/2021/08/26/sec-approves-nasdaq-comply-or-
explain-proposal-for-board-diversity/.

174 Joanna Partridge, "Number of FTSE 100 Female Directors
Rises by 50% in Five Years," *The Guardian*, February 23, 2021,
https://www.theguardian.com/business/2021/feb/23/number-
of-ftse-100-women-directors-rises-by-50-in-five-years.

175 "2010 Kenyan Constitution," § 4.2.27.8 (2010); Millicent
Omukaga, "Women on Corporate Boards: Navigating Gender

Hurdles to Access Corporate Boards in Kenya" (PhD thesis, Erasmus University Rotterdam, 2019), 3–5.

176 "Capital Markets Act," Pub. L. No. Chapter 485A, § 3.1.3.viii, 136 (2012).

177 TBR Africa Research Team, "Gender Diversity on Africa's Listed Boards: Kenya Edition," TheBoardroom Africa, April 2019; Omukaga, "Women on Corporate Boards," 3.

178 Nina Smith, "Gender Quotas on Boards of Directors," IZA World of Labor, December 4, 2018, https://wol.iza.org/uploads/articles/461/pdfs/gender-quotas-on-boards-of-directors.pdf.

179 Mark Lewis, "Most of the Women Who Make Up Norway's 'Golden Skirts' Are Non-Execs," *The Guardian*, July 1, 2011, https://www.theguardian.com/business/2011/jul/01/norway-golden-skirt-quota-boardroom.

180 Smith, "Gender Quotas on Boards of Directors."

181 "First Round 10 Year Project," First Round, accessed December 20, 2021, http://10years.firstround.com.

182 "First Round 10 Year Project."

183 Abouzahr et al., "Why Women-Owned Startups."

184 Melany Eli, "Future Looks Bright as Global VC Funding Soars to $300.5 Billion in the Second Biggest Year for VC Funding in a Decade," KPMG Global, January 20, 2021, https://home.kpmg/xx/en/home/media/press-releases/2021/01/future-looks-bright-as-global-venture-capital-funding-soars-to-usd-300-b.html; "The Global Private Equity Market Was Resilient in 2019, Capping the Best Six-Year Stretch on Record at $3.2 Trillion in Disclosed Deal Value," Cision: PR Newswire, February 24, 2020, https://www.prnewswire.com/news-releases/the-global-private-equity-market-was-resilient-in-2019—capping-the-best-six-year-stretch-on-record-at-3-2-trillion-in-disclosed-deal-value-301009451.html.

185 Bob Zider, "How Venture Capital Works," *Harvard Business Review*, November 1, 1998, https://hbr.org/1998/11/how-venture-capital-works; Deborah Gage, "The Venture Capital Secret—75% of Startups Fail," Scale Finance, accessed

December 30, 2021, https://scalefinance.com/the-venture-capital-secret-75-of-startups-fail/.

186 Henry Kanapi, "Celebrate: 5 Reasons Why Women Entrepreneurs Are Better than Men," *Hera Hub Phoenix* (blog), May 9, 2018, https://herahub.com/phoenix/celebrate-5-reasons-why-women-entrepreneurs-are-better-than-men/.

187 Adrienne LaFrance, "Why Do Women Inventors Hold So Few Patents?," *The Atlantic*, July 21, 2016, https://www.theatlantic.com/technology/archive/2016/07/the-patent-gap/492065/.

188 LaFrance, "Why Do Women Inventors?"

189 Amy Feldman, "New Study: Women Entrepreneurs Ask for Less Financing than Men, Get Smaller Loans at Higher Rates," *Forbes*, September 6, 2016, https://www.forbes.com/sites/amyfeldman/2016/09/06/new-study-women-entrepreneurs-ask-for-less-financing-than-men-get-smaller-loans-at-higher-rates/?sh=650306dd13ee.

190 LaFrance, "Why Do Women Inventors?"

191 "IFC Banking on Women Business Case Update."

192 *Women-Owned Enterprises in Vietnam: Perceptions and Potential* (International Finance Corporation, 2017), 2, https://www.ifc.org/wps/wcm/connect/86bc0493-78fa-4c7d-86ec-5858aa41fa1a/Market-study-on-Women-owned-enterprises-in-Vietnam_Eng_v1.pdf?MOD=AJPERES&CVID=l-Yi6gF.

193 *Women-Owned Enterprises in Vietnam*, 3.

194 Monish Anand, "How Women-Led SMEs Are More Reliable in Repaying Loans than Small Businesses Headed by Men," *Financial Express*, September 2, 2019, https://www.financial-express.com/industry/sme/how-women-led-smes-are-more-reliable-in-repaying-loans-than-small-businesses-headed-by-men/1693710/.

195 Anand, "How Women-Led SMEs."

196 Laurie Goodman, Jun Zhu, and Bing Bai, *Women Are Better than Men at Paying Their Mortgages* (Urban Institute, September 2016), 1, https://www.urban.org/sites/default/files/publication/84206/2000930-Women-Are-Better-Than-Men-At-Paying-Their-Mortgages.pdf.

197 Goodman, Zhu, and Bai, *Women Are Better.*

198 Kerry Rivera, "Men vs. Women: Who Wins the Credit Game?," Experian Insights, March 14, 2016, https://www.experian.com/blogs/insights/2016/03/men-vs-women-credit-trends/.

199 Rivera, "Men vs. Women."

200 Ana María Montoya et al., *Bad Taste: Gender Discrimination in the Consumer Credit Market* (Inter-American Development Bank, July 2020), 29, https://publications.iadb.org/publications/english/document/Bad-Taste-Gender-Discrimination-in-the-Consumer-Credit-Market.pdf.

201 Montoya et al., *Bad Taste.*

202 Elissa McCarter, "Women and Microfinance: Why We Should Do More," *University of Maryland Law Journal of Race, Religion, Gender and Class* 6, no. 2 (2006): 353.

203 "Why We Can Trust Women to Repay Loans," Monash University, February 26, 2020, https://www2.monash.edu/impact/articles/banking/why-we-can-trust-women-to-repay-loans/.

204 McCarter, "Women and Microfinance," 356.

205 Benjamin Robertson, Charles Daly, and Ruth McGavin, "Lack of Women Set to Cost Male-Dominated Private Equity More," *Bloomberg*, May 21, 2021, https://www.bloomberg.com/news/articles/2021-05-21/in-male-dominated-private-equity-a-lack-of-women-starts-to-hurt.

206 "The Female Face of Farming," Farming First, May 1, 2013.

207 *Mother Earth: Women and Sustainable Land Management* (United Nations Development Programme, December 1, 2015), 13, https://www.undp.org/publications/mother-earth-women-and-sustainable-land-management.

208 "Women for the Land," American Farmland Trust, accessed December 21, 2021, https://farmland.org/project/women-for-the-land/.

209 "Female Face of Farming."

210 *Mother Earth*, 13.

211 "Female Face of Farming."

212 "Female Face of Farming."
213 C. Leigh Anderson et al., "Economic Benefits of Empowering
    Women in Agriculture: Assumptions and Evidence," *The
    Journal of Development Studies* 57, no. 2 (June 4, 2020):
    193–208; Patty Devaney, "Applying a Gender Lens to
    Agriculture: Farmers, Leaders, and Hidden Influencers in
    the Rural Economy," Root Capital, September 3, 2014,
    https://rootcapital.org/resources/applying-a-gender-lens-to-
    agriculture-farmers-leaders-and-hidden-influencers-in-the-
    rural-economy/.
214 "Women in Agriculture Initiative: 2014 Annual Report," Root
    Capital, March 15, 2015, https://rootcapital.org/resources/
    women-agriculture-initiative-2014-annual-report/.
215 "When You Think Farmer—Think Female!," Food and
    Agriculture Organization of the United Nations, March 17,
    2021, https://www.adaptation-undp.org/when-you-think-
    farmer-think-female.
216 "Women, Backbone of Rural Societies," Food and Agriculture
    Organization of the United Nations, October 2014, https://
    www.fao.org/africa/news/detail-news/en/c/264948/.
217 Devaney, "Applying a Gender Lens."
218 Devaney, "Applying a Gender Lens," 10.
219 Anderson et al., "Economic Benefits of Empowering Women."
220 African Union Commission et al., "The Cost of Hunger in
    Africa: Social and Economic Impact of Child Undernutrition
    in Egypt, Ethiopia, Swaziland and Uganda" (Addis Ababa: UN
    Economic Commission for Africa, September 29, 2014), 163.
221 "The World Bank and Nutrition," World Bank, accessed
    December 21, 2021, https://www.worldbank.org/en/topic/
    nutrition.
222 Ephraim Nkonya, Alisher Mirzabaev, and Joachim von Braun,
    ed. "Economics of Land Degradation and Improvement: An
    Introduction and Overview," in *Economics of Land Degradation
    and Improvement: A Global Assessment for Sustainable
    Development,* (Cham: Springer International Publishing,
    2015), 1.

223 Lisa Prevost, "'She Build': Creating an All-Women Real
Estate Development Team," *The New York Times*, November
12, 2019, https://www.nytimes.com/2019/11/12/business/
women-real-estate-development.html.

224 WomenRising2030, *Better Leadership, Better World: Women
Leading for the Global Goals* (Business & Sustainable
Development Commission, March 2018), 31.

225 WomenRising2030, *Better Leadership, Better World.*

226 William Donovan, "The Origins of Socially Responsible
Investing," The Balance, April 23, 2020, https://www.
thebalance.com/a-short-history-of-socially-responsible-
investing-3025578.

227 Barrie C. Ingman, "ESG Regulation—Where to Start?,"
FactSet, April 29, 2020, https://insight.factset.com/
esg-regulation-where-to-start.

228 "Four for Women: A Framework for Evaluating Companies'
Impact on the Women They Employ," Wharton Social
Impact Initiative, accessed December 21, 2021, https://
socialimpact.wharton.upenn.edu/research-reports/reports-2/
four-for-women/.

229 Equileap, accessed December 21, 2021, https://equileap.com.

230 *Equileap & Refinitiv.*

231 *Equileap & Refinitiv.*

232 *Gender Equality Global Report & Ranking 2021* (Equileap,
2021), https://equileap.com/wp-content/uploads/2021/07/
Equileap_Global_Report_2021.pdf.

Chapter 3

233 "Chart Book: Tracking the Post-Great Recession Economy,"
Center on Budget and Policy Priorities, December 20, 2021,
https://www.cbpp.org/research/economy/tracking-the-post-
great-recession-economy.

234 "On Peter Thiel, Radical Life Extension, and the State,"
Philosophy for Life: The Website of Jules Evans, April 30,
2021, https://www.philosophyforlife.org/blog/on-peter-thiel-
radical-life-extension-and-the-state.

235 UN Office of Disaster Risk Reduction and Centre for
Research on the Epidemiology of Disasters, "The Human Cost
of Disasters: An Overview of the Last 20 Years 2000–2019,"
UN Office of Disaster Risk Reduction, October 12, 2020.

236 Richard Dobbs, James Manyika, and Jonathan Woetzel, "The
Four Global Forces Breaking All the Trends," McKinsey
Global Institute, April 1, 2015, https://www.mckinsey.com/
business-functions/strategy-and-corporate-finance/our-in-
sights/the-four-global-forces-breaking-all-the-trends.

237 International Labor Organization, "Employment in Services
(% of Total Employment) (Modeled ILO Estimate)," The
World Bank, January 29, 2021, https://data.worldbank.org/
indicator/SL.SRV.EMPL.ZS.

238 "Employment, Hours, and Earnings from the Current
Employment Statistics Survey (National): All Employees,
Thousands, Manufacturing, Seasonally Adjusted," US Bureau
of Labor Statistics, accessed January 5, 2022.

239 "Employment, Hours, and Earnings."

240 D. Augustus Anderson, "Retail Jobs Among the Most
Common Occupations," US Census Bureau, September 8,
2020, https://www.census.gov/library/stories/2020/09/profile-
of-the-retail-workforce.html.

241 Gretchen Berlin et al., "Women in the Healthcare Industry,"
McKinsey Global Institute, June 7, 2019, https://www.
mckinsey.com/industries/healthcare-systems-and-services/
our-insights/women-in-healthcare-moving-from-the-front-
lines-to-the-top-rung.

242 International Labor Organization, "Employment in Services."

243 Patricia Buckley and Rumki Majumdar, *The Services
Powerhouse: Increasingly Vital to World Economic Growth*
(Deloitte Insights, July 12, 2018), https://www2.deloitte.com/
content/dam/Deloitte/my/Documents/risk/my-risk-sdg8-the-
services-powerhouse-increasingly-vital-to-world-economic-
growth.pdf.

244 Rekha Khandelwal, "An Overview of the S&P 500 Retailers,"
Market Realist, October 16, 2019, https://marketrealist.

com/2019/10/an-overview-of-the-sp-500-retailers/; Lauren Thomas, "The Retail Industry Is Leading the Way as Women Take Over CEO Roles," *CNBC*, December 28, 2020, https:// www.cnbc.com/2020/12/28/the-retail-industry-is-leading-the-way-as-women-take-over-ceo-roles.html.

245 Khandelwal, "Overview of the S&P 500 Retailers."

246 Berlin et al., "Women in the Healthcare Industry."

247 Berlin et al., "Women in the Healthcare Industry."

248 Berlin et al., "Women in the Healthcare Industry."

249 John Podesta, "The Climate Crisis, Migration, and Refugees," Brookings Institution, July 25, 2019, https://www.brookings. edu/research/the-climate-crisis-migration-and-refugees/.

250 Podesta, "Climate Crisis, Migration, and Refugees."

251 Larry Fink, "Larry Fink's 2021 Letter to CEOs," BlackRock, accessed December 22, 2021, https://www.blackrock.com/us/ individual/2021-larry-fink-ceo-letter.

252 Adam B. Smith, "U.S. Billion-Dollar Weather and Climate Disasters, 1980–Present," NOAA National Centers for Environmental Information, 2020, https://data.globalchange. gov/dataset/gov_noaa_nodc_0209268.

253 David Titley, "Texas Cold Snap Was Not 'Unprecedented,' and It Was Inexcusably to Be Unprepared," *The Washington Post*, February 22, 2021, https://www.washingtonpost.com/ weather/2021/02/22/texas-cold-snap-predictable-foreseeable/.

254 Meg Wagner, Judson Jones, and Mike Hayes, "Power Outages and Winter Storm: Live Updates around the US," CNN, February 16, 2021, https://www.cnn.com/us/live-news/ snow-ice-storm-updates-02-16-21/h_df0d7883c00595650386 67e7a7547fcf.

255 Alejandro Martínez-Cabrera, "Texas Winter Storm Death Toll Could Be Much Higher than the State's Count, BuzzFeed Data Review Found," *Houston Public Media*, May 27, 2021, https://www.houstonpublicmedia.org/articles/news/energy-environment/2021/05/27/399291/texas-winter-storm-death-toll-could-be-much-higher-than-the-states-count-buzzfeed-data-review-found/.

256 "UN: Climate-Related Disasters Increase More than 80% over Last Four Decades," Red Cross Red Crescent Climate Centre, October 13, 2020, https://www.climatecentre.org/450/un-climate-related-disasters-increase-more-than-80-over-last-four-decades/.

257 "UN: Climate-Related Disasters Increase."

258 "Women's Empowerment in Water, Sanitation, and Hygiene," Water.org, August 7, 2020, 1.

259 "Facts and Figures: Women's Leadership and Political Participation," UN Women, January 15, 2021, https://www.unwomen.org/en/what-we-do/leadership-and-political-participation/facts-and-figures.

260 "Facts & Figures: Rural Women and the Millennium Development Goals," WomenWatch, accessed December 22, 2021, https://www.un.org/womenwatch/feature/ruralwomen/facts-figures.html.

261 International Monetary Fund, *Reaching Net Zero Emissions* (Group of 20, June 2021), 17, https://www.imf.org/external/np/g20/pdf/2021/062221.pdf.

262 Smith, "U.S. Billion-Dollar Weather and Climate Disasters."

263 Bradley Hope and Nicole Friedman, "Climate Change Is Forcing the Insurance Industry to Recalculate," *The Wall Street Journal*, October 2, 2018, https://www.wsj.com/graphics/climate-change-forcing-insurance-industry-recalculate/.

264 Hope and Friedman, "Climate Change Is Forcing."

265 DOE/Lawrence Berkeley National Laboratory, "Insurance Industry Paying Increasing Attention to Climate Change," ScienceDaily, December 13, 2012, https://www.sciencedaily.com/releases/2012/12/121213142311.htm.

266 "Household Air Pollution and Health," World Health Organization, September 22, 2021, https://www.who.int/news-room/fact-sheets/detail/household-air-pollution-and-health.

267 Charity Garland et al., "Black Carbon Cookstove Emissions: A Field Assessment of 19 Stove/Fuel Combinations," *Atmospheric Environment* 169 (August 15, 2017): 140–49.

268 "Household Air Pollution and Health."

269 *Burning Opportunity: Clean Household Energy for Health, Sustainable Development, and Wellbeing of Women and Children* (World Health Organization, 2016), vii.

270 Justin Lahart, "Detroit: Lean into Car-Market Turn," *The Wall Street Journal*, March 18, 2013.

271 United Nations, "The Global Food Crisis," in *The Global Social Crisis: Report on the World Social Situation 2011*, Economic and Social Affairs (New York: United Nations, 2011), 61.

272 Food and Agriculture Organization of the UN, *Women in Agriculture: Closing the Gender Gap for Development*, The State of Food and Agriculture 2010/11 (Rome: FAO, 2011), 38.

273 "Women Could Feed Millions More People if Given Access to Means of Production," UN News, March 7, 2011, https://news.un.org/en/story/2011/03/368252-women-could-feed-millions-more-people-if-given-access-means-production-un.

274 Katherine Schaeffer, "Women Do More Cooking, Grocery Shopping than Men Among U.S. Couples," Pew Research Center, September 24, 2019, https://www.pewresearch.org/fact-tank/2019/09/24/among-u-s-couples-women-do-more-cooking-and-grocery-shopping-than-men/.

275 *Danone Climate Policy* (Danone, 2020), 6, https://www.danone.com/content/dam/danone-corp/danone-com/about-us-impact/policies-and-commitments/en/2016/2016_05_18_ClimatePolicyFullVersion.pdf.

276 "Mission: The Creamery of Tomorrow," Miyoko's Creamery, accessed December 22, 2021, https://miyokos.com/pages/mission-creamery-of-tomorrow.

277 Mathieu Boniol et al., "Gender Equity in the Health Workforce: Analysis of 104 Countries," World Health Organization, 2019, https://apps.who.int/iris/handle/10665/311314.

278 Jack Zenger and Joseph Folkman, "Research: Women Are Better Leaders During a Crisis," *Harvard Business Review*, December 30, 2020, https://hbr.org/2020/12/research-women-are-better-leaders-during-a-crisis.

279 O'Donnell, "Meet the Women at Forefront."

280 Institute for Economics and Peace, "Global Peace Index 2016," ReliefWeb, June 8, 2016.

281 Max Roser, "War and Peace," Our World in Data, December 13, 2016, https://ourworldindata.org/war-and-peace.

282 "Women's Participation in Peace Processes," Council on Foreign Relations, accessed December 23, 2021, https://www.cfr.org/womens-participation-in-peace-processes/; "Women's Participation and a Better Understanding of the Political," Global Study on the Implementation of UN Security Council Resolution 1325, accessed December 30, 2021, https://wps.unwomen.org/participation/.

283 Nick Noel et al., "The Economic Impact of Closing the Racial Wealth Gap," McKinsey & Company, August 13, 2019, https://www.mckinsey.com/industries/public-and-social-sector/our-insights/the-economic-impact-of-closing-the-racial-wealth-gap.

284 "Gender-Based Violence (Violence Against Women and Girls)," World Bank, September 25, 2019, https://www.worldbank.org/en/topic/socialsustainability/brief/violence-against-women-and-girls.

285 "Gender-Based Violence."

286 Lakshmi Puri, "The Economic Costs of Violence Against Women," UN Women, September 21, 2016, https://www.unwomen.org/en/news/stories/2016/9/speech-by-lakshmi-puri-on-economic-costs-of-violence-against-women.

287 Puri, "Economic Costs of Violence Against Women."

288 Puri, "Economic Costs of Violence Against Women."

289 Robin Chase, *Peers Inc: How People and Platforms Are Inventing the Collaborative Economy and Reinventing Capitalism*, Kindle ed. (New York: PublicAffairs, 2015).

290 "Whose Time to Care: Unpaid Care and Domestic Work during COVID-19," UN Women, November 25, 2020, https://data.unwomen.org/publications/whose-time-care-unpaid-care-and-domestic-work-during-covid-19.

291 "Women in the Workplace 2021," McKinsey & Company, September 27, 2021, https://www.mckinsey.com/

featured-insights/diversity-and-inclusion/women-in-the-workplace.

292 "Women in the Workplace 2021."

293 Courtney Connley, "Women's Ambition Plummeted During the Coronavirus Pandemic, as Careers Stalled and Burnout Spiked," CNBC, March 9, 2021, https://www.cnbc.com/2021/03/09/65percent-of-working-women-say-pandemic-has-made-things-worse-at-work.html.

294 Avie Schneider, Andrea Hsu, and Scott Horsley, "Multiple Demands Causing Women to Abandon Workforce," *Weekend Edition Saturday*, NPR, October 2, 2020, https://www.npr.org/sections/coronavirus-live-updates/2020/10/02/919517914/enough-already-multiple-demands-causing-women-to-abandon-workforce.

295 "Women in the Workplace 2021."

296 Bovino and Gold, "Key to Unlocking?"

Chapter 4

297 Rhymer Rigby, "We All Have Worries but Those of the Rich Are Somehow Different," *Financial Times*, February 26, 2019, https://www.ft.com/content/b2e56c96-1f32-11e9-a46f-08f9738d6b2b.

298 "Global Soft Power Index 2020," BrandFinance, 2020, https://brandirectory.com/globalsoftpower/.

299 "Global Soft Power Index 2020."

300 "Global Soft Power Index 2020."

301 "Global Soft Power Index 2020."

302 "Political Risk Insurance," National Association of Insurance Commissioners, February 25, 2021.

303 "Over Two-Thirds (68%) of Firms Have Suffered a Political Risk Loss, Willis Towers Watson Survey Finds," Willis Towers Watson, December 5, 2019, https://www.wtwco.com/en-US/News/2019/12/over-two-thirds-of-firms-have-suffered-a-political-risk-loss-willis-towers-watson-survey-finds.

304 "Allianz Risk Barometer 2021—Political Risks and Violence," Allianz Global Corporate & Specialty, January 19, 2021,

https://www.agcs.allianz.com/news-and-insights/expert-risk-articles/allianz-risk-barometer-2021-political-risks.html.

305 "Civil Unrest Index," Verisk Maplecroft, accessed December 23, 2021, https://www.maplecroft.com/risk-indices/civil-unrest-index/.

306 Maria Elena Vizcaino, "Goldman Tells Investors to Bet on Gender Equality for Bigger Bond Returns," *Bloomberg*, December 1, 2021, https://www.bloomberg.com/news/articles/2021-12-01/goldman-says-betting-on-gender-equality-pays-bigger-bond-returns.

307 "Sixth Assessment Report: Climate Change 2021: The Physical Science Basis," IPCC, August 9, 2021, https://www.ipcc.ch/assessment-report/ar6/.

308 Jocelyn L Knoll and Shannon L. Bjorklund, *Force Majeure and Climate Change: What Is the New Normal?* (Dorsey & Whitney LLP, March 4, 2020), https://www.dorsey.com/-/media/files/uploads/images/force_majeure_and_climate_change_030420.pdf?la=en.

309 "New Study Sheds Light on Angel Investors in the US Economy," Harvard Business School, November 30, 2017, https://www.hbs.edu/news/releases/Pages/angel-investors-us-economy.aspx.

310 "New Study Sheds Light."

311 Ilya A. Strebulaev and Will Gornall, "How Much Does Venture Capital Drive the U.S. Economy?," Stanford Graduate School of Business, October 21, 2015, https://www.gsb.stanford.edu/insights/how-much-does-venture-capital-drive-us-economy.

312 Maria Ben, "Role of Venture Capital in the Economic Growth of United States," ABC Investments, August 14, 2019, https://medium.com/@abc_40376/role-of-venture-capital-in-the-economic-growth-of-united-states-11b2090330a1.

313 TrueBridge Capital, "Female Investors Shine on 2021 Midas List Despite Difficult Year," *Forbes*, April 13, 2021, https://www.forbes.com/sites/truebridge/2021/04/13/female-investors-shine-on-2021-midas-list-despite-difficult-

year/?sh=6b857f684f51.

314 Abeyta, "Women Now Make Up."

315 Gompers and Kovvali, "Other Diversity Dividend."

316 "All Raise All In: Women in the VC Ecosystem," PitchBook, November 11, 2019, https://pitchbook.com/news/reports/2019-pitchbook-all-raise-all-in-women-in-the-vc-ecosystem.

317 "The Untapped Potential of Women-Led Funds," Women in VC, October 2020, https://assets.ctfassets.net/jh572x5wd4r0/7qRourAWPj0U9R7MN5nWgy/711a6d-8344bcd4fbe0f1a6dcf766a3c0/WVC_Report_-_The_Untapped_Potential_of_Women-Led_Funds.pdf; Ashley Bittner and Brigette Lau, "Women-Led Startups Received Just 2.3% of VC Funding in 2020," *Harvard Business Review*, February 25, 2021, https://hbr.org/2021/02/women-led-startups-received-just-2-3-of-vc-funding-in-2020; Ben Bergman, "2020 Was Great for Startups, if You Were a Man," dot.LA, April 27, 2021, https://dot.la/all-raise-2020-report-2652799431.html.

318 *The Female Leadership Crisis: Why Women Are Leaving (and What We Can Do About It)* (Network of Executive Women, 2016), 4, https://businessdocbox.com/Human_Resources/78347015-The-female-leadership-crisis-why-women-are-leaving-and-what-we-can-do-about-it.html.

319 *Female Leadership Crisis*, 5.

320 *Female Leadership Crisis*, 8.

321 Julia Boorstin, "Survey: It's Still Tough to Be a Woman on Wall Street—but Men Don't Always Notice," CNBC, June 26, 2018, https://www.cnbc.com/2018/06/25/surveyon-wall-street-workplace-biases-persist—-but-men-dont-see-t.html.

322 "Statistics on the Purchasing Power of Women," Girl Power Marketing, 2020, https://girlpowermarketing.com/statistics-purchasing-power-women/.

323 "Statistics on the Purchasing Power of Women."

324 Yvonne Lin, "The Innovation Economy Is Terrible at Designing for Women," *Fast Company*, September 20, 2016,

https://www.fastcompany.com/3063442/the-innovation-economy-is-terrible-at-designing-for-women.

325 Michael J. Silverstein and Kate Sayre, "The Female Economy," *Harvard Business Review*, September 1, 2009, https://hbr.org/2009/09/the-female-economy.

326 Bridget Brennan, *Winning Her Business* (New York: HarperCollins Leadership, 2019).

327 Silverstein and Sayre, "Female Economy."

328 "Why 80% of Women Leave Their Advisors When They Lose Their Husband," *Advisorpedia*, March 15, 2017, https://www.advisorpedia.com/advisor-tools/why-80-of-women-leave-their-advisors-when-they-lose-their-husband/; Judy Paradi and Paulette Filion, "Why Women Leave Their Financial Advisors: And How to Prevent It," StrategyMarketing.ca, https://www.strategymarketing.ca/wp-content/uploads/Why-women-leave-their-financial-advisors-and-how-to-prevent-it.pdf; Ilana Polyak, "For Some Widows, Breaking Up with an Advisor Is Easy to Do," *CNBC*, October 11, 2014, https://www.cnbc.com/2014/10/10/husbands-gone-widows-part-ways-with-advisors-too.html.

329 "29 CFR § 1604.11—Sexual Harassment" (1999).

330 Lynn Parramore, "$MeToo: The Economic Cost of Sexual Harassment," Institute for New Economic Thinking, January 2018, https://www.ineteconomics.org/research/research-papers/metoo-the-economic-cost-of-sexual-harassment.

331 Parmita Das, "$MeToo," *Berkeley Economic Review*, November 22, 2018, https://econreview.berkeley.edu/metoo/.

332 Mads Borelli-Kjaer, Laurids Moehl Schack, and Ulf Nielsson, "#MeToo: Sexual Harassment and Company Value," *Journal of Corporate Finance* 67 (April 1, 2021).

333 Shiu-Yik Au, Ming Dong, and Andreanne Tremblay, "Employee Sexual Harassment Reviews and Firm Value," SSRN Scholarly Paper (Rochester, NY: Social Science Research Network, August 17, 2019), 1.

334 *The Economic Costs of Sexual Harassment in the Workplace* (Deloitte Access Economics, March 2019), 6, https://

www2.deloitte.com/content/dam/Deloitte/au/Documents/
Economics/deloitte-au-economic-costs-sexual-harassment-
workplace-240320.pdf.

335 Parramore, "$MeToo."

336 Ute Krudewagen, "Harassment Policies & Training Around
the Globe," *Emtrain: People Leader Blog* (blog), December
9, 2020, https://emtrain.com/blog/sexual-harassment/
international-training/; "Sexual Harassment Training Now
Required in Six States," *Traliant: Compliance Blog* (blog),
January 2, 2020, https://www.traliant.com/blog/sexual-
harassment-training-now-required-in-six-states/.

337 Sarah Kaplan, "Anti-Sexual Harassment Training: Does
It Work?," Gender and the Economy, December 11, 2019,
https://www.gendereconomy.org/anti-sexual-harassment-
training-does-it-work/.

338 Christy Glass, Alison Cook, and Brandon Pierce, "Do Women
in Leadership Reduce Sexual Harassment Claims on College
Campuses?," *Journal of Women and Gender in Higher Education*
13, no. 2 (May 3, 2020): 193–210.

339 Au, Dong, and Tremblay, "Employee Sexual Harassment
Reviews."

340 Au, Dong, and Tremblay, "Employee Sexual Harassment
Reviews."

341 *Hidden Value: The Business Case For Reproductive Health* (Rhia
Ventures, January 2020), https://rhiaventures.org/wp-content/
uploads/2020/01/Hidden-Value_The-Business-Case-for-
Reproductive-Health.pdf.

342 Serena G. Sohrab and Nada Basir, "Employers, It's Time to
Talk About Infertility," *Harvard Business Review*, November
11, 2020, https://hbr.org/2020/11/employers-its-time-to-
talk-about-infertility; "FP2020 Family Planning's Return
on Investment," FP2030, https://fp2030.org/resources/
fp2020-family-plannings-return-investment; *Maternity Care
in the United States: We Can—and Must—Do Better* (National
Partnership for Women & Families, February 2020), https://
www.nationalpartnership.org/our-work/resources/health-care/

maternity-care-in-the-united.pdf.

343 "COVID-19's Impact on Women's Employment," McKinsey & Company, March 8, 2021, https://www.mckinsey.com/ featured-insights/diversity-and-inclusion/seven-charts-that-show-covid-19s-impact-on-womens-employment.

344 Roosa Tikkanen et al., "Maternal Mortality and Maternity Care in the United States Compared to 10 Other Developed Countries," CommonWealth Fund, November 18, 2020, https://www.commonwealthfund.org/publications/ issue-briefs/2020/nov/maternal-mortality-materni-ty-care-us-compared-10-countries.

345 Marian F. MacDorman et al., "Is the United States Maternal Mortality Rate Increasing? Disentangling Trends from Measurement Issues," *Obstetrics and Gynecology* 128, no. 3 (September 2016).

346 "What Does 'Top Talent' Think About Working in States That Ban Abortion?," Perry Undem, August 31, 2021, https:// docplayer.net/220733760-What-does-top-talent-think-about-working-in-states-that-ban-abortion-reactions-to-texas-new-abortion-ban.html.

347 Maggie McGrath, "Survey: Two Thirds of College-Educated Workers May Avoid Texas Because Of Abortion Ban," *Forbes*, September 2, 2021, https://www.forbes.com/sites/ maggiemcgrath/2021/09/02/survey-two-thirds-of-college-educated-workers—may-avoid-texas-because-of—abortion-ban/?sh=fab98f06e4c0.

348 "Costs of Reproductive Health Restrictions," Institute for Women's Policy Research, 2021, https://iwpr.org/costs-of-reproductive-health-restrictions/.

349 Family Health Outcomes Project, *The Business Case for Promoting Healthy Pregnancy* (University of California, San Francisco, n.d.), 3, https://fhop.ucsf.edu/sites/fhop.ucsf.edu/ files/custom_download/The%20business%20case%20for%20 promoting%20health%20pregnancy.pdf.

350 CDC, "Breastfeeding FAQs," Centers for Disease Control and Prevention, August 10, 2021.

351 "The Business Case for Breastfeeding: Steps for Creating a Breastfeeding Friendly Worksite," Department of Health and Human Services, Health Resources and Services Association, 2008.

Chapter 5

352 Emma Hinchliffe, "The 'Care Economy' Is a $648 Billion Opportunity, Melinda French Gates' Pivotal Ventures Found," *Fortune*, July 14, 2021, https://fortune.com/2021/07/14/melinda-french-gates-pivotal-ventures-care-economy-648-billion/.

353 Robert Jenkins, "Why We Need More Female Teachers Across All Levels of Education," *UNICEF Connect* (blog), October 4, 2019, https://blogs.unicef.org/blog/need-more-female-teachers-across-levels-education/; "The Care Economy," The Community Foundation for Greater New Haven, accessed December 23, 2021, https://www.cfgnh.org/articles/the-care-economy.

354 "Not All Gaps Are Created Equal: The True Value of Care Work," Oxfam International, January 20, 2020.

355 "ILO: 90 Percent of Domestic Workers Excluded from Social Protection," International Labour Organization, March 14, 2016, https://www.ilo.org/beirut/media-centre/news/WCMS_458878/lang—en/index.htm.

356 Rebecca Boone, "Idaho Lawmaker Draws Ire After Saying Moms Should Stay Home," *U.S. News & World Report*, June 3, 2021, https://www.usnews.com/news/politics/articles/2021-03-03/idaho-lawmaker-draws-ire-after-saying-moms-should-stay-home.

357 "Education All Around Us," Shaping Tomorrow, October 18, 2018, https://www.shapingtomorrow.com/home/alert/6264466-Education-All-Around-Us.

358 Cynthia Hess, Tanima Ahmed, and Jeff Hayes, *Providing Unpaid Household and Care Work in the United States: Uncovering Inequality* (Institute for Women's Policy Research, January 2020), 2, https://iwpr.org/iwpr-issues/esme/

providing-unpaid-household-and-care-work-in-the-united-
states-uncovering-inequality/.

359 Kyle Alspach, "Care.Com Closes IPO with $104.6 Million
Raised; Shares up 61% Since 1st Day," *Boston Business Journal*,
January 30, 2014, https://www.bizjournals.com/boston/blog/
techflash/2014/01/carecom-closes-ipo-at-1046-million.html.

360 *Building Education Systems Fit for the 21st Century*, The
Changemakers Series, Women of the World Endowment,
2021.

361 Careship, accessed January 5, 2022, https://www.careship.de.

362 Heather Timmons and Andrea Shalal, "Analysis: How
Biden Plans to Add $600 Billion to the U.S. 'Care
Economy,'" Reuters, May 6, 2021, https://www.reuters.
com/world/us/how-biden-plans-add-600-billion-us-care-
economy-2021-05-06/.

363 Peter L. Singer, *Federally Supported Innovations: 22 Examples
of Major Technology Advances That Stem from Federal Research
Support* (The Information Technology & Innovation
Foundation, February 2014), https://www2.itif.org/2014-fed-
erally-supported-innovations.pdf.

364 "ILO Calls for Urgent Action to Prevent Looming Global
Care Crisis," International Labour Organization, June 28,
2018, https://www.ilo.org/global/about-the-ilo/newsroom/
news/WCMS_633115/lang—en/index.htm.

365 Isabella Breda, "How Norway Built an Economy That
Puts People First," *YES! Magazine*, November 3, 2020,
https://www.yesmagazine.org/issue/what-the-rest-of-the-
world-knows/2020/11/03/how-norway-built-an-economy-
that-puts-people-first.

366 Helen Penn, *Report for SOW on the Financing of Early
Childhood Education and Care in Europe, and, in Particular,
on the Training and Remuneration of Childcare Workers and
Its Costs* (National Academies of Sciences, Engineering,
and Medicine, September 2017), 28, https://sites.nation-
alacademies.org/cs/groups/dbassesite/documents/webpage/
dbasse_186435.pdf.

367 David Nikel, "Parental Leave & Other Benefits in Norway," Life in Norway, November 18, 2021, https://www. lifeinnorway.net/parental-leave/.

368 Penn, *Report for SOW*.

369 Roosa Tikkanen and Melinda K. Abrams, "U.S. Health Care from a Global Perspective, 2019: Higher Spending, Worse Outcomes?," The Commonwealth Fund, January 30, 2020, https://www.commonwealthfund.org/publications/ issue-briefs/2020/jan/us-health-care-global-perspective-2019.

370 Berlin et al., "Women in the Healthcare Industry."

371 Jacqueline LaPointe, "Nearly 71% of Practice Revenue Under Fee-For-Service in 2016," *RevCycle Intelligence*, December 27, 2017, https://revcycleintelligence.com/news/nearly-71-of-practice-revenue-under-fee-for-service-in-2016.

372 LaPointe, "Nearly 71% of Practice Revenue."

373 Rachel K. Jones and Jenna Jerman, "Population Group Abortion Rates and Lifetime Incidence of Abortion: United States, 2008–2014," *American Journal of Public Health*, November 8, 2017.

374 "Costs of Reproductive Health Restrictions."

375 Tara O'Neill Hayes and Rosie Delk, "Understanding the Social Determinants of Health," American Action Forum, September 4, 2018, https://www.americanactionforum.org/ research/understanding-the-social-determinants-of-health/.

376 Hayes and Delk, "Understanding the Social Determinants of Health."

377 Helen E. Jack et al., "Impact of Community Health Workers on Use of Healthcare Services in the United States: A Systematic Review," *Journal of General Internal Medicine* 32, no. 3 (March 2017): 325–44; Kelsey Vaughan et al., "Costs and Cost-Effectiveness of Community Health Workers: Evidence from a Literature Review," *Human Resources for Health* 13, no. 1 (September 1, 2015); "Penn's Community Health Worker Program Yields $2.47 for Every $1 Invested Annually by Medicaid," Penn Medicine News, February 7, 2020, https://www.pennmedicine.org/news/

news-releases/2020/february/penns-community-health-worker-program-yields-247-for-every-1-invested-annually-by-medicaid.

378 "Contraceptive Use in the United States by Method," Guttmacher Institute, May 2021, https://www.guttmacher.org/fact-sheet/contraceptive-method-use-united-states.

379 "Contraceptive Total Market U.S. 2014–2025," Statista, January 2020, https://www.statista.com/statistics/1085669/contraceptive-total-market-size-us/.

380 "Unintended Pregnancy," Centers for Disease Control, July 20, 2021, https://www.cdc.gov/reproductivehealth/contraception/unintendedpregnancy/index.htm.

381 Michelle Osterman et al., "Births: Final Data for 2020," National Center for Health Statistics (U.S.), February 7, 2021.

382 Andrew Hurst, "The Cost of a C-Section Is More than $9,000 Greater on Average than a Vaginal Delivery," ValuePenguin, May 3, 2021, https://www.valuepenguin.com/cost-of-vaginal-births-vs-c-sections.

383 Richard E. Behrman, Adrienne Stith Butler, and Institute of Medicine (US) Committee on Understanding Premature Birth and Assuring Healthy Outcomes, *Societal Costs of Preterm Birth*, *Preterm Birth: Causes, Consequences, and Prevention* (Washington, DC: National Academies Press, 2007).

384 Donna L. Hoyert, "Maternal Mortality Rates in the United States, 2019," National Center for Health Statistics (U.S.), June 10, 2021.

385 Gianna Melillo, "US Ranks Worst in Maternal Care, Mortality Compared with 10 Other Developed Nations," *American Journal of Managed Care*, December 3, 2020, https://www.ajmc.com/view/us-ranks-worst-in-maternal-care-mortality-compared-with-10-other-developed-nations.

386 "Estimates of Funding for Various Research, Condition, and Disease Categories (RCDC)," National Institutes of Health RePORT, June 25, 2021, https://report.nih.gov/funding/categorical-spending#/.

387 Muhammad Atif et al., "Does Board Gender Diversity Affect

Renewable Energy Consumption?," *Journal of Corporate Finance* 66 (February 1, 2021).

388 Mary Halton, "Climate Change 'Impacts Women More than Men,'" BBC News, March 8, 2018, https://www.bbc.com/news/science-environment-43294221.

389 Betty Hearn Morrow and Elaine Enarson, "Hurricane Andrew Through Women's Eyes: Issues and Recommendations," *International Journal of Mass Emergencies and Disasters* 14, no. 1 (March 1996): 5.

390 E. Enarson and B. Morrow, "Women Will Rebuild Miami: A Case Study of Feminist Response to Disaster," in *The Gendered Terrain of Disaster* (Westport, CT: Greenwood Publication, 2006), 174–76.

391 Enarson and Morrow, "Women Will Rebuild Miami," 74.

392 Enarson and Morrow, "Women Will Rebuild Miami," 176.

393 Enarson and Morrow, "Women Will Rebuild Miami," 178.

394 Joe McCarthy, "Understanding Why Climate Change Impacts Women More than Men," Global Citizen, March 5, 2020, https://www.globalcitizen.org/en/content/how-climate-change-affects-women/.

395 Phudoma Lama, Mo Hamza, and Misse Wester, "Gendered Dimensions of Migration in Relation to Climate Change," *Climate and Development* 13, no. 4 (April 21, 2021): 326–36.

396 Mary Robinson, *Climate Justice: A Man-Made Problem with a Feminist Solution* (New York: Bloomsbury, 2018).

397 Zoe Tabary, "Climate Change A 'Man-Made Problem with A Feminist Solution' Says Robinson," Reuters, June 18, 2018, https://www.reuters.com/article/us-global-climatechange-women/climate-change-a-man-made-problem-with-a-feminist-solution-says-robinson-idUSKBN1JE2IN.

398 Robinson, *Climate Justice,* 106.

399 "1 Million Women," accessed December 24, 2021, https://www.1millionwomen.com.au.

400 Chattopadhyay and Duflo, "Women as Policy Makers."

401 chrome-extension://efaidnbmnnnibpcajpcglclefindmkaj/viewer.html?pdfurl=https%3A%2F%2Fwww.fao.

org%2F3%2Fi2050e%2Fi2050e.pdf&clen=3493976

402 "Empowering Women Farmers to End Hunger and Poverty," Oxfam International, October 12, 2017, https://www.oxfam. org/en/empowering-women-farmers-end-hunger-and-poverty.

403 Vanessa Nakate, "Ugandan Activist Vanessa Nakate: Why I Launched a One-Woman Protest Against Climate Change," Global Citizen, February 12, 2020, https://www.globalcitizen. org/en/content/vanessa-nakate-climate-activism-in-africa/.

404 Anya Kamenetz, "'You Need To Act Now': Meet 4 Girls Working to Save the Warming World," *Morning Edition*, NPR, January 19, 2020, https://www.npr. org/2020/01/19/797298179/you-need-to-act-now-meet-4-girls-working-to-save-the-warming-world.

405 Joan Michelson, "ESG Investing Is a Star. Women Are Why," *Forbes*, March 16, 2021, https://www.forbes.com/sites/joanmi-chelson2/2021/03/16/esg-investing-is-a-star-women-are-why/?sh=784ea6ea4bde.

406 Michelson, "ESG Investing Is a Star."

407 "Sustainable Investing Basics," The Forum for Sustainable and Responsible Investment, accessed December 24, 2021.

408 "Sustainable Investing Basics."

409 "Sustainable Reality: Analyzing Risk and Returns of Sustainable Funds," Morgan Stanley Institute for Sustainable Investing, 2019, 1.

410 "Sustainable Reality."

411 Alastair Marsh, "Responsible Investing Is a Rare Field of Finance Led by Women. Now It's Hot—and Men Want In," *Fortune*, January 24, 2020, https://fortune.com/2020/01/24/responsible-esg-investing-women-finance/.

412 Fink, "Larry Fink's 2021 Letter to CEOs."

413 Alexandre Di Miceli and Angela Donaggio, *Women in Business Leadership Boost ESG Performance: Existing Body of Evidence Makes Compelling Case* (International Finance Corporation, Washington, DC, 2018), 4, https://www.ifc.org/wps/wcm/connect/21ab518b-dfc8-4ec2-82b7-c5653a366ce9/PSO42. pdf?MOD=AJPERES&CVID=muo7s9y.

414 *Gender Diversity and Climate Innovation* (The Sasakawa Peace
    Foundation, December 1, 2020), 8, https://www.spf.org/en/
    gender/publications/20201201.html.

415 WomenRising2030, *Better Leadership, Better World.*

416 Xiaoyan Zhou et al., "The Effect of Firm-Level ESG Practices
    on Macroeconomic Performance," *SSRN Electronic Journal,*
    June 3, 2020.

417 "New Study Lays Out Opportunities to Slash Land-Based
    GHG Emissions from Forests, Farming, and Consumer
    Behavior," Project Drawdown, October 13, 2021, https://
    drawdown.org/news/insights/new-study-lays-out-opportuni-
    ties-to-slash-land-based-ghg-emissions-from-forests; Stephanie
    Roe et al., "Land-Based Measures to Mitigate Climate Change:
    Potential and Feasibility by Country," *Global Change Biology*
    27 (2021): 6025–58.

418 "The Changemaker Series: Converting Natural Asset
    Value to Financial Capital," Women of the World
    Endowment, October 22, 2021, https://www.youtube.com/
    watch?v=yY5tQy2guAE.

419 Anne Boden, "Why We Need to #MAKEMONEYEQUAL,"
    Starling Bank (blog), March 13, 2018, https://www.
    starlingbank.com/blog/make-money-equal/.

420 Boden, "Why We Need to #MAKEMONEYEQUAL."

421 "Microcredit: One of the Best Ways of Empowering Women,"
    The Borgen Project (blog), September 16, 2020, https://borgen-
    project.org/microcredit-empower-women-econ/.

422 Garick Giroir, "How Men and Women Spend Their Money
    Differently," Louisiana Federal Credit Union, January 6, 2020,
    https://www.louisianafcu.org/articles/how-men-and-women-
    spend-their-money-differently.

423 "Vanguard Examines 401(k) Behavior/Outcome Gender
    Paradox."

424 "Who's the Better Investor, Men or Women?," Fidelity, May
    18, 2017, https://www.fidelity.com/about-fidelity/individu-
    al-investing/better-investor-men-or-women/.

425 "Quick Facts About the Gender Wage Gap," Center for

American Progress, March 24, 2020, https://www.american-progress.org/article/quick-facts-gender-wage-gap/.

426 Shelly Schwartz, "Women Lagging in Retirement Saving: Survey," CNBC, March 4, 2015, https://www.cnbc.com/2015/03/04/women-lagging-in-retirement-saving-survey.html.

427 Kim Eberhard, "The Super Legacy of Bank's First Females," Westpac Wire, March 8, 2018, https://www.westpac.com.au/news/in-depth/2018/03/the-super-legacy-of-banks-first-females/.

428 "Who's the Better Investor, Men or Women?"

429 "How Men And Women Manage Money Differently," *Acclaim Federal Credit Union* (blog), January 21, 2020, https://www.acclaimfcu.org/how-men-and-women-manage-money-differently/.

430 Geri Stengel, "University Of New Hampshire Creates Pipeline Of Women Venture Capitalists," *Forbes*, May 19, 2021, https://www.forbes.com/sites/geristengel/2021/05/19/university-of-new-hampshire-creates-pipeline-of-women-venture-capitalists/?sh=469d821a5845.

431 "Women, Investing & the Pursuit of Wealth-Life Balance," Pacific Investment Management Company LLC, accessed December 24, 2021, https://www.pimco.com/en-us/our-firm/diverse-perspectives/wealth-life-balance.

432 Eberhard, "Super Legacy of Bank's First Females."

433 Carole Comerton-Forde et al., *Using Survey and Banking Data to Measure Financial Wellbeing* (Melbourne Institute of Applied Economic and Social Research, March 2018), 25, https://fbe.unimelb.edu.au/__data/assets/pdf_file/0005/2839433/CBA_MI_Tech_Report_No_1_Chapters_1_to_6.pdf; "How Men And Women Manage Money Differently."

434 Monica Costa, Marian Sawer, and Rhonda Sharp, "Women Acting for Women: Gender-Responsive Budgeting in Timor-Leste," *International Feminist Journal of Politics* 15, no. 3 (September 12, 2012).

435 Inga Hajdarowicz, "Does Participation Empower? The

Example of Women Involved in Participatory Budgeting in Medellin," *Journal of Urban Affairs*, March 5, 2018.

436 Hajdarowicz, "Does Participation Empower?"

437 David H. Freedman, "How Medellín, Colombia, Became the World's Smartest City," *Newsweek*, November 18, 2019, https://www.newsweek.com/2019/11/22/medellin-colombia-worlds-smartest-city-1471521.html.

438 "Who's the Better Investor, Men or Women?"

439 Brad M. Barber and Terrance Odean, "Boys Will Be Boys: Gender, Overconfidence, and Common Stock Investment," *Quarterly Journal of Economics*, February 2001, 261–92.

440 Pippa Stevens, "Women-Managed Funds Are Outperforming as Tech Exposure Pays Off, Goldman Finds," CNBC, August 31, 2020, https://www.cnbc.com/2020/08/31/women-managed-funds-are-outperforming-as-tech-exposure-pays-off-goldman-finds.html.

441 *How America Saves 2020* (Vanguard, June 2020), 92, https://institutional.vanguard.com/ngiam/assets/pdf/has/how-america-saves-report-2020.pdf.

442 Barber and Odean, "Boys Will Be Boys."

443 "Predicting Long-Term Success for Corporations and Investors Worldwide," FCLTGlobal, September 29, 2019, https://www.fcltglobal.org/resource/predicting-long-term-success-for-corporations-and-investors-worldwide/.

444 "Predicting Long-Term Success."

445 "World's Largest Retirement Funds in 2021"; Kirakosian, "World's Largest Asset Owner Invests €2.4bn in Gender Diversity Index."

446 *Plenary Discussion: Stepping Up for Systems Change*, Panel Discussion, Gender Smart Investing Summit, 2021.

447 David Runacres, "Why Is Japan Embracing ESG Investing?," *Refinitiv Perspectives* (blog), July 19, 2021; "FTSE Blossom Japan Index," FTSE Russell, accessed December 26, 2021, https://www.ftserussell.com/products/indices/blossom-japan.

448 Khalid Azizuddin, "Japan's Government Pension Fund Unveils $12bn Allocation to Global ESG and Gender Equity

Indices," Responsible Investor, December 18, 2020, https://www.responsible-investor.com/articles/japan-s-government-pension-fund-unveils-usd12bn-allocation-to-global-esg-and-gender-equity-indices; Sarah Min, "GPIF Invests $12.5 Billion in Morningstar, MSCI ESG Benchmarks," Chief Investment Officer, December 21, 2020, https://www.ai-cio.com/news/gpif-invests-12-5-billion-morningstar-msci-esg-benchmarks/.

449 *Plenary Discussion: Stepping Up for Systems Change.*

450 Henderson et al., "Should a Pension Fund Try to Change the World?"

451 Henderson et al., "Should a Pension Fund Try to Change the World?"

452 *Plenary Discussion: Stepping Up for Systems Change.*

453 *Plenary Discussion: Stepping Up for Systems Change.*

454 Daniel Brooksbank, "Japan's Government Pension Fund Joins Boardroom Diversity Initiatives in UK and US," Responsible Investor, November 11, 2016, https://www.responsible-investor.com/articles/gpif-30.

455 Min, "GPIF Invests $12.5 Billion in Morningstar, MSCI ESG Benchmarks."

456 Brooksbank, "Japan's Government Pension Fund."

Chapter 6

457 Abouzahr et al., "Why Women-Owned Startups."

458 Goodman, Zhu, and Bai, *Women Are Better.*

459 Anthony Martinez and Cheridan Christnacht, "Women Are Nearly Half of U.S. Workforce but Only 27% of STEM Workers," Census.gov, January 26, 2021, https://www.census.gov/library/stories/2021/01/women-making-gains-in-stem-occupations-but-still-underrepresented.html.

460 Cassie Werber, "Company Boards Need at Least Three Women Before They Truly Begin to Change," *Quartz*, December 11, 2018, https://qz.com/work/1490993/company-boards-need-three-women-before-they-truly-begin-to-change/.

461 Sarah O'Brien, "How to Recruit More Women to Your Company," *Harvard Business Review*, November 28, 2019,

https://hbr.org/2019/11/how-to-recruit-more-women-to-your-company.

462 "Four for Women."

463 O'Brien, "How to Recruit More Women."

464 Julia Enyart, "Gender Lens Investing in Public Markets: It's More than Women at the Top," Glenmede, January 6, 2021, https://www.glenmede.com/insights/gender-lens-investing-public-markets-more-than-women-at-top/.

465 Esther K. Choo et al., "The Development of Best Practice Recommendations to Support the Hiring, Recruitment, and Advancement of Women Physicians in Emergency Medicine," *Academic Emergency Medicine* 23, no. 11 (June 11, 2016): 1203–9.

466 *Shaping the Future Together: Male Champions for Gender Equity: Experiences, Drivers and Lessons Learned* (Ernst & Young, 2014), https://archive.bio.org/sites/default/files/docs/toolkit/EY%20Shaping%20the%20Future%20Together.pdf.

467 David G. Smith and W. Brad Johnson, *Good Guys: How Men Can Be Better Allies for Women in the Workplace* (Boston: Harvard Business Review Press, 2020).

468 Smith and Johnson, *Good Guys.*

469 "Four for Women."

470 Joyce Ehrlinger and David Dunning, "How Chronic Self-Views Influence (and Potentially Mislead) Estimates of Performance," *Journal of Personality and Social Psychology* 84 (February 1, 2003): 5–17.

471 Michelle Ryan and S. Haslam, "The Glass Cliff: Evidence That Women Are Over-Represented in Precarious Leadership Positions," *British Journal of Management* 16, no. 2 (June 1, 2005).

472 Jaclyn Trop, "Is Mary Barra Standing on a 'Glass Cliff'?," *The New Yorker*, April 29, 2014, https://www.newyorker.com/business/currency/is-mary-barra-standing-on-a-glass-cliff.

473 Ryan and Haslam, "Glass Cliff."

474 Tamara Keith, "Best Way to Get Women to Run for Office? Ask Repeatedly," *All Things Considered*, NPR, May 5, 2014,

https://www.npr.org/2014/05/05/309832898/best-way-to-get-women-to-run-for-office-ask-repeatedly.

475 "Visualizing the Data: Women's Representation in Society," UN Women, February 25, 2020, https://www.unwomen.org/en/digital-library/multimedia/2020/2/infographic-visualizing-the-data-womens-representation.

476 "Visualizing the Data."

477 "Women on Corporate Boards (Quick Take)," Catalyst, November 5, 2021, https://www.catalyst.org/research/women-on-corporate-boards/.

478 Smith and Johnson, *Good Guys*.

479 Smith and Johnson, *Good Guys*.

480 Werber, "Company Boards Need."

Epilogue

481 Sushmita Pathak, "Village Teacher Wins $1 Million Prize For World's Most 'Exceptional' Educator," NPR, February 12, 2021, https://www.npr.org/sections/goatsandsoda/2021/02/12/966835697/village-teacher-wins-1-million-prize-for-worlds-most-exceptional-educator.

482 "Current Term Enrollment Estimates," National Student Clearinghouse Research Center, June 10, 2021, https://nscresearchcenter.org; Kevin Carey, "Men Fall Behind in College Enrollment. Women Still Play Catch-Up at Work," *The New York Times*, September 9, 2021, https://www.nytimes.com/2021/09/09/upshot/college-admissions-men.html.

483 Ari Levy, "Minorities and Women Are Finally Getting a Seat at the IPO Underwriting Table," CNBC, August 14, 2021, https://www.cnbc.com/2021/08/14/ipo-underwriting-mwvbe-investment-firms-getting-seat-at-the-table.html.

INDEX